SUPERWOMAN
DOESN'T LIVE HERE ANYMORE!

Judith Neumann-Dicks

authorHOUSE

AuthorHouse™
1663 Liberty Drive
Bloomington, IN 47403
www.authorhouse.com
Phone: 1-800-839-8640

© 2009 Judith Neumann-Dicks. All rights reserved.

No part of this book may be reproduced, stored in a retrieval system, or transmitted by any means without the written permission of the author.

First published by AuthorHouse 11/5/2009

ISBN: 978-1-4490-4941-6 (e)
ISBN: 978-1-4490-2783-4 (sc)

Printed in the United States of America
Bloomington, Indiana

This book is printed on acid-free paper.

Dedication

To my mother,

for her unconditional love and support in whatever I did in life. I could never out give her loving ways.

Table of Contents

Purpose Of This Book		xi
Chapter 1.	The Dirty Little Secret	1
Chapter 2.	Afterwards	6
Chapter 3.	Bob	10
Chapter 4.	Spouse No. 2	17
Chapter 5.	David	21
Chapter 6.	Marrying Bob	29
Chapter 7.	Niame	34
Chapter 8.	Getting Settled with Bob	36
Chapter 9.	The House from Hell	39
Chapter 10.	A Perfect Storm on the Horizon	46
Chapter 11.	Contributing Factors	54
Chapter 12.	A Look Back	68
Chapter 13.	Miscarriages	93
Chapter 14.	The Storm Builds	95
Chapter 15.	Another Look Back	100
Chapter 16.	More Military Memories	107
Chapter 17.	Jacob Is Born	114

Chapter 18.	A Fresh Start	124
Chapter 19.	Jim	128
Chapter 20.	Remarrying Bob	136
Chapter 21.	Bob's Cancer	146
Chapter 22.	Bob's Background	160
Chapter 23.	Early Painful Memories	166
Chapter 24.	Daddy Dies	180
Chapter 25.	Len	184
Chapter 26.	My Religious Beliefs	198
Chapter 27.	Mother	200
Chapter 28.	Miracles	222
Chapter 29.	Marie	235
Chapter 30.	Al, Ward, and Joyce	240
Chapter 31.	Richard	248
Chapter 32.	Jacob	254
Chapter 33.	The Last Vacation	258
Chapter 34.	Deaths	272
Chapter 35.	No More Superwoman	282
Judith Neumann-Dicks		285
Superwoman Doesn't Live Here Anymore		287

Recognition

A special thanks to the following for their teachings:

Pastor John Sale

Grace Community Bible Church

Roselle, Illinois

Pastor David Riemenschneider and Pastor Bill Calvin

Bloomingdale Missionary Alliance Church

Bloomingdale, Illinois

Special thanks also to Joe Schrantz of Villa Park,
Illinois, for his assistance in writing this book.
I owe him more than words can express.

Purpose Of This Book

The purpose of this book is to share my life story so that it may help others who are walking along one or more of the pathways I have traveled.

I want to let you, the reader, know that no matter what you are going through, there is *Hope,* that God is there for you all of the time as your closest friend.

As this book attests, I went through some very dark moments, some of which include the following:

- raped when I was in my twenties
- the birth of a son who had early health problems
- the birth of twins, in which I almost died, with one of the babies stillborn
- three miscarriages
- three divorces
- the deaths of various relatives and close friends

I want you to know that you, too, can have a personal relationship with God. This personal relationship will sustain you through your hard times.

This I know from experience. All throughout my life, God was always there, protecting me. Even when I made bad decisions, God protected me.

He knew my life before I was born. He set my path but allowed me to make my own decisions. I didn't always choose what was right. That wasn't God's fault; that was *my* fault. But when I veered off the right path, I got back up, dusted myself off, and got back on course.

Yes, there is hope. Yes, there is ALWAYS hope. God is always there close to you wanting to be your best friend. Even when you neglect him, he is always there, waiting.

I know from the bottom of my heart that I want to live my life to glorify the Lord so that when I die, when he comes, I want him to find me on the path where he put me.

In addition to various dark moments, I have also had many joyful times. And I learned from experience that the closer I walk with God, the more joyful my life becomes.

I've even experienced miracles. Yes, *miracles.* (Miraculous answers to prayer.) Nothing is too great for our God to accomplish. *Nothing.* You, too, can experience miracles.

Yes, God is first in my life. He is my heavenly Father. He wants me to receive good gifts, and when I ask for help, he gives it.

With God being my number one priority, my second priority is my husband. My third priority is my children and the rest of my family.

Life is so very short that it seems a shame not to put your priorities in order. Is it so important not to put church activities or organizations ahead of your family, or a Tupperware or home-decorating party before your husband? Don't do it!

What are my other priorities? *Love* towers over everything. Next is *honesty* -- in all things. Money means nothing.

How do I stay close to God? The answer is simple: through *prayer*.

How do I pray? If I have a real concern, I will pray every chance I get. Sometimes even, praying without ceasing.

My prayer might be, "Lord, I give this up to you. I can't carry this burden. I leave it at your feet. You promised me you wouldn't give me more than I can handle." Hear it is, I can't handle it.

He never has, and he never will. God keeps his word.

Sometimes I will tell him, "It is way too heavy for me. Besides, you are up 24 hours a day. This is what I'm asking, and this is what I need."

I like to pray every day with Len, my dear spouse. One night he starts, and the next night, I start. We pray for family, friends, and various groups with which we are affiliated. Our prayer might go something like the following:

"Thank-you, Lord, for this beautiful day. Thank-you for all you have given us. We ask for forgiveness of sins. We pray for our families, for our grief-support group, our Seniors Club, its President, the Addison Police Department, children in wheelchairs, our friends in Florida, Kitty and her boys, our acquaintances who are sick, and those close friends whom we know need special prayers. In the Name of Jesus, we pray. Amen."

When do I feel closest to God? Only during a crisis? No, because I can and often do feel very close to God even when there is no crisis in my life. When you draw near to God, God will draw near to you. Even when you are in the midst of a battle, you can have peace and joy.

This bears repeating:

Even when you are in the midst of a battle, you can have peace and joy.

Yes, it's true. No problem, no battle, no situation, *nothing* is too big for our God. He's there by your side. He wants to be your best friend.

Trust in the Lord with all your heart, and you can survive anything. In your darkest hour, he will be there for you.

What are a few other "rules" I follow in my walk with God? Among the most important are:

- Do not judge. As you judge, God will judge you.
- Forgive at all times in *every* area of your life. If you won't forgive others, God won't forgive you.
- God has shown me that anger and bitterness have no room in the heart of the godly. Give up *all* anger and bitterness so that you can be a new creation in Christ.
- Use whatever talents you have for God's glory. Not for your glory.
- Counsel with God, and you will see your every need being met instead of living in a prison or an unhealthy body due to what is self-inflicted.
- Talk to God often in prayer. I do so at least several times a day, no matter what the situation. When something serious occurs, I'll pray more often. Remember: prayer is essentially talking with God -- communicating with God. But *don't do all the talking; remember to listen.*

Here is an example of the power of prayer: One day a lady came to Addison Seniors Club burdened with family troubles. She and I were the only two at our table. As we started to talk, she began to tell me all that was troubling her.

I said, "That's a pretty big load to carry. Would you like for me to pray with you and ask the Lord to lift it off you?"

She said, "Yes", and we joined hands, and I prayed. No one around us even noticed. When I finished, I hugged her. I said, "Start your day by asking the Lord to help you make it through that day. Then at night, be sure to thank him for that day."

A week later she came back and said, "You won't believe how much better my week went. I can't believe it. God does indeed make a difference."

Here is another example: My son Jacob went on a camping trip into Mexico with a friend. It worried me because this was before cell phones, and I would have no way to reach him. Before going to bed for the night, I asked the Lord to protect them.

At four o'clock in the morning I awoke filled with anxiety for Jacob. I sat up in bed and said, "What is it, Lord? If it's Jacob, send your angels and please don't let anything happen to him."

Then I went back to sleep. At six-thirty, I awoke again. But this time I felt at peace.

Jacob called the next day. He said, "You wouldn't believe what happened last night."

I said, "Stop. Tell me if I'm right. It was at four o'clock in the morning, wasn't it?"

He said, "Yes. How did you know? We were on a road that leads up a mountain. It started snowing, and we couldn't see anything. We made it to the top, and there was a motel. We checked into the motel and went to bed. When we got up later that morning, we looked down the mountain. We were shocked. It's a miracle we hadn't driven over the edge of that road."

I told him, "God woke me at four o'clock, and I asked him to send his angels to protect you."

Another example: My brother Ward lives in Mexico and had come down with E. coli. He and a friend had been out to dinner on a Sunday evening, and the friend was also stricken. By Tuesday, his friend was dead. About that same day I received a call from Ward's landlord. He said Ward was terribly ill, and he asked if he should take him to the hospital. I said by all means.

I started praying for Ward. And I prayed. And I prayed morning, noon, and night. First, I asked the Lord to save him. Second, I asked the Lord to prevent his organs from shutting down. Third, I asked the Lord whether or not I should go to Mexico to be with him. The Lord said No. Fourth, I asked the Lord if I should send him money. The Lord said, "Yes". Fifth, I asked the Lord to show me whom to trust and whom not to trust. He did. Sixth, I asked the Lord if I should hire help. He said, "Yes".

The result: Ward recovered. He lost 30 pounds, but was able to come home in August of 2008 to see his family.

Yet, another example: My brother Al has a bad heart and has undergone three or four open-heart surgeries. He is a diabetic and has lost a leg. They want to remove the other one, but they know he won't survive the surgery. He had pneumonia, and he thought for sure he would die. He phoned and we talked about it. I never stopped praying. I couldn't sleep, so I wrote him a loving good-bye letter, telling him how much he means to me. We had a family reunion on August 2, 2008, and Al was here for it. He turned 72 on August 3.

Another example: My friend Arlene called one day and asked if I would pray for her husband. He was going through back surgery, and it was touch-and-go as to whether or not he would ever walk again. I told her I would meet her at the hospital.

I met Arlene and her husband's daughter in an empty waiting room. We closed our eyes and began to pray. Before we had finished praying, a woman entered the room and when we were finished, she asked if we would pray for her husband. The room kept filling, each new arrival asked us to pray, and we kept praying. We prayed for the Lord to guide the doctor's hands.

Arlene's husband recovered and not only walked again, but also went back to his job as a carpenter.

I love to pray for people. Before going to sleep, I tell the Lord, "Please wake me if you want me to pray for someone." And, he does. I often wake in the middle of the night feeling directed to pray for a particular person.

I also pray with people every Sunday at services in the Bloomingdale Missionary Alliance Church, Bloomingdale, Illinois.

Do I read the Bible? Yes, I do, very much so that I am on my third *Lindsell Study Bible*. I wore out the first two. Yes, *wore them out!* As I read, I underline verses that I feel are important to me. In fact, our pastor is making an outline each week with every verse we look up and write, and what we get out of it, and how it applies to our lives. You see, the Bible was written back in Jesus' time, but history repeats; there are lots of lessons for today.

What are my favorite Bible verses? Here are some of them (from the *Lindsell Study Bible*):

- *2 Corinthians 5*: This tells how we gain new heavenly bodies.

- *Proverbs 18-22*: A man who finds a wife gets a special blessing from the Lord.

- *Proverbs 16-3*: Commit your work to the Lord. Then it will succeed.

- *Proverbs 13:24*: If you refuse to discipline your son, it proves you don't love him, for if you love him, you will be prompted to punish him.

- *Psalm 147:3*: He heals the broken-hearted, binding up their wounds.

How often do I read the Bible? Four to five times a week, sometimes just a verse, sometimes a chapter. When I hear the verses at our Sunday worship services, I have already looked them up during the week. I don't like to take what is said without proof. If I find it in my Bible, then it becomes real to me. I am fortunate to have a pastor who truly believes in the Bible as the inspired word of God, and to sit under his teachings. If God says it, I believe it. If man says it, I look it up.

What is my personal relationship with Jesus? I came to Jesus and asked him to clean out my heart. I asked him to clean up my life and to put my feet on the right path so I may take up whatever I have in order to follow him.

I said to myself, "If Jesus were to return today or tomorrow, I wouldn't want him to find me in a place where I shouldn't be. So I stay out of there. I want Jesus to know: I'm on his team."

In which part of my life did I feel closest to God?

"I would say the five years of Bob's cancer. Bob was my second husband. But we divorced, and I married a third time, but that marriage ended up in divorce after five months. Then I married Bob again.

"When we first found out he had cancer, we went home and laid in bed and embraced each other. He was 48, and I was 46. We Prayed

Chapter 1

The Dirty Little Secret

I met Roy through a friend. When I spotted the gun on his waist, I was very uneasy until I found out he was a State Police officer. He was wearing a sport coat and gray pants. He looked clean, neat, and he was very tall, somewhat balding. He spoke well and was funny. When he asked me out, I felt comfortable with him.

Our first date was to a local restaurant. Fine dining, good conversation. I was impressed. He talked about his job, and I talked about my boys and my job. He brought me home and gave me a quick kiss at the front door.

A week or two later he phoned and apologized for not calling sooner. He said he had been very busy at work. I thought nothing of it. He asked me to go flying with him. He said we would stop for lunch.

It wasn't until our third date that we went flying. When he pointed out his house down below, I was surprised at the size of it. What single man lives in a four- or five-bedroom house alone? Is this guy married and just looking for a little fling on the side? My attitude about him suddenly changed. Not only was it a clear day for flying, but I, too, could see more clearly now. I knew at that moment I would never go out with him again.

A month or so passed and Roy didn't call. This is when Bob came into my life and took me flying -- but without a plane. My every thought through the day began to be filled with Bob. He and I were meant to be. It was only two weeks since we met (there was no ring), but in another two weeks we would go to downtown Chicago on the train to a justice of the peace.

That first month Bob would come home to my boys and me at my apartment, and we would have dinner together every night. He would go home about midnight and come by at 6 o'clock in the morning. I would have coffee made, and we would start our day over coffee and a kiss. Then he would go off to work. We would soon marry.

The phone rang, and it was Roy.

"I see your boyfriend left," he said.

How did he know about Bob? Was I being watched?

"I'm next door at the White Hen, and I'm coming over."

"Don't. I can't see you anymore. I'm getting married in two weeks."

"I'm coming anyway. You better open the door or I'll wake the neighbors."

I had just gotten up out of bed and had on a robe, a nightgown, and panties.

Now he's at the door rapping loudly on the knocker. I ran to the door, and there he stood. He looked *so* big.

"You shouldn't be here," I told him right away. "But now that you are, I'm getting married in two weeks."

He was very angry. I didn't understand why. If I had meant that much to him, why hadn't he called? I was just as glad he hadn't.

He looked at me and put his hands on my upper arms, pushing me backwards . . . down the hall . . . past the boys' room.

"Stop. Stop it. You'll wake my boys."

My nails are digging into the molding in the hallway.

"No. No. Don't do this," I managed to say.

He was silent, but his angry face told me his intentions.

At the end of the hall was my bedroom, with a four-poster bed. He pushed me onto it and jumped on top of me, pinning me to the bed.

He ripped off my underpants. I knew what was about to happen, but I couldn't stop him. My anger was at the bursting point. I cried out, "Lord, help me."

That's when I shut down. I didn't fight back, but I wasn't going to contribute either. I lay there as though dead.

He never said another word. When he finished, he left.

I figured, when I hadn't contributed, it had to take the joy out of it.

I got up, double-locked the front door and watched him drive off.

I burst into tears and stood there shaking.

I can't call the police. They would never arrest one of their own. And even if they did, he would be out in no time, back here to kill me.

I was glad my boys were still asleep.

I got into the bathtub and tried to wash him off me. I was crying and I wanted to scream. But that would wake the boys.

My tears were silent. That day changed my life. I had lived through a RAPE.

I couldn't bring myself to tell Bob. I was worried about him, because Roy knew his car. Would he try anything with him? Or was it really over?

Lord, protect Bob; protect my kids; protect me. Don't ever let him come back.

I never saw him again.

The only person I ever told was Dr. Green three years later. During those three years, it ate at me; I lived in fear.

My cute little figure went out of control. If I were fat, no one would ever look at me sexually again.

I didn't go anywhere after dark alone. When I would hear of a rape on TV, I wanted to be the hanging judge. I was armed and ready. This would never happen to me again. Lord help the man who tried. Lay silent? No way. I would make more noise than a fire alarm.

It was only six months before we moved away from there . . . eighteen months before my heart attack . . . three years before I started seeing Dr. Green.

I locked doors all the time. I looked in my rearview mirror and didn't put up with prank calls.

I knew it wasn't my fault. I knew it was an act of *control* and *violence*. After all, I had been Superwoman before (I could do it all), and no one was going to take that away from me. God had given me my super power, and only he would take it away.

Chapter 2

Afterwards

The next evening Bob helped me again to put the boys to bed. He had brought along a rented movie for us to watch.

"You seem awfully quiet Judy. Anything wrong? You feeling okay?"

I forced a smile.

"I'm fine. Maybe tired. I did have a busy day showing my apartment to some prospects. Richard and Jacob were a handful."

The inner voice was still shrieking, like a Halloween monster cavorting about seeking attention. If only I could tell Bob. If only I could tell Sandy. If only I could tell someone. Anyone.

"Maybe the movie will cheer you up. It's supposed to be a comedy. Lots of laughs."

He put an arm around me. If only I could tell him. It was an Abbott and Costello movie. Whenever Abbott spoke, probably because he was taller than Costello, I kept seeing Roy. But there the resemblance ended.

Abbott was mild-mannered; Roy was mean. If I had only known he had such a mean, violent streak -- like a Jekyll and Hyde.

I wish I could show Bob my upper arms. Bruise marks on each where Roy grabbed me. On the outside of each arm were four bruises, one for each finger, and near each underarm, a bruise from his thumb. My God, he squeezed me tightly. I can still feel the pain.

Bob let out intermittent bursts of laughter. I faked a few laughs. Roy had been so rough and mean. Never once during my years of marriage to David had he ever been violent. He was always gentle, especially making love.

The inner voice shrieked again. *I've been raped! I've been raped! I've been raped!* I choked back a sob.

"Judy, what's the matter?"

"N . . . n . . . nothing. I'm . . . all . . . right. Maybe I'm coming down with something. I feel awfully tired."

If I could only tell him. If I could only tell anyone.

Bob kissed my cheek and held me tightly.

"Want me to turn off the movie and leave so you can get some rest?"

"No. Don't leave. Stay here. I'll be all right."

I thought about my sister, Joyce. Maybe I could tell her. After all, what are sisters for? I thought of my mother. Could I tell her? No. Never. That would be too embarrassing. Joyce . . . maybe.

When Bob kissed me on my lips, the shrieking subsided. Costello did a pratfall. I actually laughed.

"There. I think you're feeling better."

He kissed my lips again.

I thought more about Bob's and my likes and dislikes. I became conscious of his Old Spice smell. He's active in the Church, and so am I. We're in agreement in politics -- we're both Republicans.

I liked his handsome profile, his tan skin coloring, and what a talented musician. He plays the trumpet, accordion, and keyboard. Three instruments!

I found myself laughing at more jokes. The shrieking shrank to a dull hum.

Then I saw Roy's face on the screen again. Should I go to the police and turn him in? Never. The story would get in the paper. Besides, he would deny it. It would be my story against his. Maybe I could tell Bob's father, now a retired Chicago cop. No. That also would be too embarrassing.

I shivered. I thought about what Roy did in his police work. He was on a *bomb* squad. I cringed. If I went public, he'd blow up my apartment, killing the boys and me. I shuddered.

"Are you cold?" Bob asked.

"A trifle. Maybe I'm coming down with a cold."

He kissed me again on the lips.

I thought about trying to get Roy arrested. Put in jail. Getting a police officer to arrest another police officer? Was I crazy? Would never happen.

I said a silent prayer. Dear God, you know what happened. It's our secret. It's our secret.

The humming seemed to grow louder.

Chapter 3
Bob

I had supper with my boys -- macaroni and cheese. Dropped them off again with Sandy. I had a date that night with Bob. We took in a movie, and we returned to my apartment. I rounded up Richard and Jacob.

"Hi, big guys. Who wants the first piggyback ride?" Bob asked.

"I do," screamed Richard.

"No, I do," shouted Jacob.

"Whoa. Wait a minute. I can take only one at a time. Okay. Richard, you went first last time. It's Jacob's turn to go first."

Half a dozen piggyback rides later, Bob helped me put the boys to bed.

A bit later we were sitting on the sofa watching the TV news. That is, the TV was turned on, but we were busy doing other things.

I had been seeing Bob off and on for almost a month. But lately things seemed to be getting serious.

Bob reached into his pocket and pulled out a small box. My heart skipped a beat. I quickly opened it.

"Oh, Bob! It's beautiful."

"It's a whole carat."

He kissed me.

"Judy, will you marry me?"

He kissed me again.

"Oh, Bob. Yes."

We kissed again.

Ironically, Bob had been divorced for two years, same as me. He also had two boys the same age as mine. We also had a lot of common interests. We like to ski and dance. Plus, when we were born in Chicago, we had lived on the same street only six blocks apart. And probably the strangest part of all, Bob's father was the Chicago policeman crossing guard at my school when I was in kindergarten.

I had recently started asking God to bring me a husband. I had more than a bit of help from a ladies Bible study that had been meeting in my apartment for over a year. I had asked them to meet there so I wouldn't have to get a babysitter for Rich and Jacob.

I had mentioned to the ladies several times that, although I was dating and had lots of friends, maybe, just maybe, I could use a husband who could be a father for my boys. One evening the ladies said they were going to pray for the Lord to find a husband for me. I said, Okay, half-heartedly.

Two weeks later I opened the front door of my apartment, which doubled as my office for managing the 10 buildings and 136 apartments. *There stood the answer to their prayers.*

He was tall and thin, and wore a tan leather jacket, brown pants that were bell-bottoms that flared out over his tan western boots. His face was thin. He had clean, clear, bright-blue eyes, with a smile that showed his beautiful teeth. His hair was brown around a three-inch circular bald top. I liked the smell of his after-shave lotion. The sunlight in the hallway was making him glow, or maybe it was the crystal chandelier.

I stepped back and gestured for him to come in. "Welcome," I said, "how can I help you?"

"Hi. I'm Bob Neumann. I've lived here for two years, and I'm here to sign my new lease."

My mind was rushing with, where had he been hiding? Why hadn't we met?

"I don't think we've met," I said.

"Actually, we have met. I had locked myself out of my apartment on a Thursday night and I needed to get to the bank. So you ran over and let me in."

Then I remembered. We both had been in a rush. I was hurrying to pick up Jacob from day care right behind the apartment complex.

He signed his lease, and we talked for two hours in my living room. He was a Christian. He didn't smoke or drink -- only on occasion. He was divorced and in addition to having two boys the same age as mine, he was actively involved in their lives. Besides skiing and dancing, he enjoyed boating, photography, music, and he went to church weekly.

We made two dates that day; the first one was for dinner and dancing.

He came at 7 o'clock on a Friday night. I had worked all day and had to go to the corporate office in Park Ridge. The complex was in Schaumburg on Springinsguth Road. It was after six by the time I got back. I hopped into the tub and put my hair in hot rollers. I had dried and dressed and was pulling the rollers, throwing them toward my bedroom door as the front door knocker started banging against the metal plate.

My hair was blonde and shoulder-length, now hanging in ringlets, uncombed. No makeup, which didn't much matter, I mainly just wore lipstick. I weighed in at 110 pounds.

This time he was standing in the door with a tan sport coat, tan pants, and brown shoes, smiling and smelling just as good as he had the other day. I was a wreck from rushing around; he was as calm as could be.

"I've never seen the model apartment. Could I?" My mind flashed. Is it clean? I thought about the rollers. "Sure."

I gave him the same lines that I gave everyone on the tour, until we got to the rollers. "Our manager has a date tonight and hasn't had time to take out these rollers yet. Please excuse her." We both laughed.

The model apartment had two bedrooms, one bath, walk-in closets, living room, dining room, kitchen, patio or balcony, and laundry area on the second floor. The hallway had a front and back entrance, red brick walls in the hall, red carpet, and see-through stairs and two large crystal chandeliers at each entrance of four units.

The families who lived there took pride in adhering to the building rules. I have to admit, I loved my job.

As he toured the apartment, we got to the bedroom door, and he stopped and said, "Let's get this out of the way."

He placed his hands on both sides of my face and leaned in with a kiss. It really knocked me for a loop. I hadn't ever been kissed like that. *Yep, God sent him all right.*

We left for dinner to a restaurant on River Road in Schiller Park, just a few blocks from where he worked at Wisconsin Tool and Stamping Company. The dance floor was made of Plexiglas. There were oranges and lemons and limes overlapping each other with lights under them. The dining room was on the other end. All throughout the meal, which was delicious, we talked nonstop.

We moved to the dance floor. There was a balcony about four feet higher than the dance floor. *He could dance.* We were Fred Astaire and Ginger Rogers.

The evening ended, and I had a hard time sleeping, rehashing all that had transpired, wondering -- Is he feeling the way I'm feeling?

He called early Saturday morning to thank me for a wonderful evening. He said he was picking up his boys and taking them to Twin Lakes, Wisconsin, where his parents lived. He was teaching his boys to ski and to play the trumpet. His mother lavished love on the boys; his dad was quiet but also loved them. They were their only grandchildren.

Our next date was going to be on Monday, April 26, his birthday. I cooked up a storm over the weekend. I knew the way to a man's heart. He liked oriental food, and I knew how to cook it. A girlfriend had taught me four years earlier.

The following week I took Bob's lease to the main office, McLennon and Company, out of Park Ridge. I said to my boss: "Could you delay signing this lease. I have bigger and better plans for this guy."

He told me to hold onto it until I wanted him to sign it.

Why hadn't I prayed for a husband earlier? Surely, Bob and I would be a marriage made in heaven.

The first thing next morning I took the boys with me to Sandy's apartment to show her my ring.

"Sandy, isn't it beautiful? Bob asked me to marry him. It's a full carat."

"He did? Oh, Judy. Did you say yes?"

"I sure did."

"You really love him?"

"I do. We both enjoy the same things. I've known him for a short time, and I know he's the right one. We attend the same church. He's kind and thoughtful. It'll be a perfect match."

Sandy hugged me.

"I'm so happy for you. Will you continue living here in the complex?"

"Yes. To start, anyway."

Only six weeks had passed, and we would be married soon. It had been 18 months since my divorce from David Largo, my children's father. David had already married Carol.

Bob and I stayed married for twenty four almost twenty five years with a three year break after seven years. The last seventeen years were the most wonderful years with God leading our path.

Chapter 4

Spouse No. 2

It was Friday, the day before I was going to marry Bob Neumann. We decided that after we married, he would move in with me in my apartment. He told me to go over to his apartment and set aside anything I thought we could use, and we could pack it up later.

I went to his apartment while Bob was away at work. Unlocking and opening the door, I thought, so this is what he has been coming home to for the last two years. In the living room a long, nondescript, drab-green sofa was against a wall, with a coffee table, also nondescript, in front of it.

In the dining room was a large walnut desk with pictures of his sons on top, along with his trumpet, which he said was his prized possession. It was highly polished and took center stage.

Turning the corner into the kitchen, I saw a card table and three chairs. The fourth chair was behind the desk.

I opened each kitchen cabinet drawer and the cabinet door.

"Oh, my God!"

Everything was neatly arranged (Exactly in place.) Canned goods were in alphabetical order; vegetables and soups were all in a line, like soldiers.

The refrigerator was clean but contained little food. After all, we had been eating out or at my apartment.

I went into the bedroom. There was the bedroom set he had picked out after his divorce. I thought it was the ugliest bedroom set I had ever seen. It was a Spanish style with a red velvet inlay and lots of turnings on the bed. Candles were on the nightstands. I smiled because this hinted to me that he had a romantic side.

Although we both had been married and were not strangers to sex, being Christians, we had decided to put it off until our honeymoon. We had kissed and snuggled, but nothing more. This was likely the reason we decided to marry after having known each other for only a month.

The linen closet and bathroom were highly organized and clean.

I left his apartment in a panic. I was marrying a *"neatnik"*. Me . . . Judy Faye Smith Largo, was definitely not in that category. I'm not a slob, but a *neat freak*? No way!

I had to work that day in my capacity as manager of the apartment complex. Sandy, my sister-in-law, was coming to pick up my boys. And my friends were giving me a bachelorette party. Bob and I had agreed not to see each other until 9 o'clock Saturday morning.

I closed the office at 5 o'clock. I no sooner fed my boys than Sandy arrived. She was married to my brother Ward and was my best friend. They had five children.

She was going to take Rich and Jacob to her apartment and return them after Bob and I were married. Then my friends started arriving. I told the boys, "When you come home, Bob is going to move in and live with us and be a daddy to you. Bob's boys, Rusty and Robbie, will become your new brothers."

My Jacob and Bob's Rusty were both two, and my Richard and his Robbie were both six. All four were as cute as could be, and they all got along well. I had complete custody of my boys; Bob had a shared-custody arrangement with his ex-wife, getting his boys on weekends.

My four girlfriends were ready to party and asked where I wanted to go. But I had other plans.

"I know this is going to shock you, but, really, rather than go out for a party, I'd like you to stay here and help me." I laughed. "You see, Bob had me inspect his apartment today and pick out anything I thought we could use." I laughed again. "I learned that Bob is a "neatnik", and that's definitely not one of my attributes. Instead of going out, would you all mind staying here and helping me tidy up? Get things straightened out so Bob won't be so shocked when he moves in with me and the boys?"

They agreed. There were four closets, the kitchen and bathroom cabinets, two dressers, and a desk to straighten out. With five of us, how hard could that be?

Each selected a drawer or a cabinet to clean out and rearrange. I put out the snacks and rounded up the vodka, Galliano, and orange juice to make Harvey Wall-bangers. I had some vanilla ice cream in the freezer to blend in. There would be time to party after the work was done.

Judith Neumann-Dicks

My apartment was basically clean, that is, on the surface. After all, I resided in the complex's model apartment. It had to look neat at all times so I could show it to prospective renters at a moment's notice. But the disarray *inside* the drawers and cabinets was another matter.

A few hours later we were done. We did it! We had had a lot of laughs. Now I wouldn't have to worry. My new "neatnik" husband won't be shocked.

As I sat back and relaxed to enjoy our party, I became aware that I hadn't been thinking about the rape. I silently thanked God.

Saturday morning, my wedding day, I got up early. It was a sunny June day. I swear I could feel my blood pumping much faster than usual. The pit of my stomach was turning flips.

I curled my hair and put on my makeup. Looking at myself in the mirror, I thought of David, my first husband.

"If you would have been good to me, you never would have lost out on me," I mumbled.

Chapter 5
David

When David and I became engaged, I was finishing high school.

When I had turned 16, Mrs. Largo, David's mother, had told me about a waitress job where she worked. She had trained me. Tips were good. I worked part-time after school and averaged $22 in tips a day. My father had taught me to sew, and this would play out in many areas of my life. Jobs came easy. I was soon working in management in a better class of ladies wear. Then came the artist job in California. I had the world by the tail. *Superwoman lives.*

David had given me an engagement ring, which he had originally given to Sharon, his girlfriend before me. The ring was a cubic zirconium imitation diamond. I wasn't at all proud of it. It had the peculiar characteristic of *clouding up* in the daylight. We had shopped for a new ring but couldn't afford one. Unbeknownst to me, David had put on layaway a ring I had admired.

David was working fulltime in the pharmacy at Sears and taking night classes at Wright Junior College. This had told me he was ambitious. He had indeed talked the good talk with hopes and dreams and goals. David was a salesman; and I was sold.

One afternoon he came to my mother's house. He was off from work that day, and I had just gotten home from school. We were sitting on the turquoise blue sofa in front of our big picture window in the living room.

"I'm going to need that ring back that you've been wearing," he said abruptly.

My heart sank; my eyes welled up. I slipped the ring off and handed it to him, not saying a word. I couldn't. I didn't even look up.

"Because I want you to have your own ring." He pulled a small cubic box out of his pocket.

I should have been elated. But how could my emotions rise up so quickly from rock bottom? This should have told me that this is not the man to marry. (A light bulb moment.) How could he be so cruel? But me, I put the ring on and married him a few months later. I never told anyone of that lame proposal. I wasn't very proud of that moment.

I graduated from high school that June in 1964. David and I were wed Sept. 26. I was 18; he was 20. It was a cool; fall evening on a Friday night. The wedding was planned for 7 o'clock in the pastor's office, with family and a few friends present. Since I was six years old, I had attended Irving Park Baptist Church on Irving Park Road in Chicago. The pastor was Rev. Bill Mayers, a soft-spoken, tall, dark-headed, good-looking man.

David, in his suit, was tall and very good-looking. He had a warm smile with perfect teeth, brown eyes, with dark blond hair with streaks of light blond on the curls. He stood about six-one, and weighed about 165 pounds, with not an ounce of fat. The suit fit him perfectly.

I was five-five and weighted 107 pounds. I had no chest and a long neck and wore glasses. I didn't feel very pretty, but he said I was.

Diana, his sister, was my maid of honor, and David's close friend, Lance, was the best man.

I had asked my dad to give me away. That is, only if it were important enough for him that he would not drink that day. He came and gave me away. He had always told me I was special. I was so proud of him that he had remained sober for my wedding.

My wedding dress was a two-piece white dress I could wear for any occasion. I went to the train station and bought $3 worth of flowers. You could buy a bunch of flowers for a dollar. I went home and made a bouquet and a corsage for both mothers and for the maid of honor. I made boutonnieres for the two fathers, the groom, and the best man. I baked and decorated the cake. I made my own veil. The total amount I spent on the wedding: $50.

David was very neat when it came to his appearance. The Sears pharmacy where he worked was at Six Corners in Chicago (Irving Park, Milwaukee Avenue, and Cicero). He had to wear a fresh white uniform shirt with black trousers, which made him look like a doctor.

He didn't wear jeans like the other guys; he always wore dress pants. When we would go on a date, he would wear a suit. He always liked to go downtown to the better restaurants and movie theaters.

He didn't own a car until just before we got married. It was an old Chevy that broke down more often than it ran. Soon after we were married, he bought an old Cadillac. Being color-blind, he thought it was beige, but actually, it was pink. The Cadillac also had problems; it would often overheat.

David's mother gave a shower for us at a hall; over a hundred people came. By the time the shower was over, the only thing we needed was groceries. We set up housekeeping with the few things we owned and with all the gifts from the shower. The only thing we lacked was money so we could get the gas turned on.

For our honeymoon, David and I drove to a fishing cabin next to Loon Lake in southern Illinois. I remember it as a honeymoon from hell.

The car broke down before we left Chicago. We stayed at David's aunt's house, and his cousin ran into the house very early in the morning without knocking.

Loon Lake was located in the middle of a wooded area. While I slept, David got up early and went fishing.

The car broke down again, and we had no money for a motel.

When we got back from the honeymoon, we went out and bought new furniture and had more bills than the mailbox could handle. Due to unforeseen problems with the car, we had no money for a deposit to get the gas turned on. It got cold early that year. Thank God for all those beautiful gift blankets.

We had vowed to each other that we would not run home and ask for money. We would make it on our own or do without.

We did without for one month. No heat, no hot water, no gas to cook with. We took baths at my mother's. I heated water on a hot plate for him to shave each morning. Supper was one-pot meals on the hot plate. Somehow we survived that first month.

When we finally had the deposit for the gas company, they told us, "Oh, you actually didn't need a deposit, because he had been working at the same job for over two years."

My great dislike for camping probably originated in the way David and I "camped out" in that apartment for the first month.

While David worked at Sears, I worked across the street at Foyers; a shop that sold better dresses. My boss, was a short, round, gray-haired Jewish man. He was so sweet to me. He once said I was the daughter he never had. His beautiful wife was a model. Their son was going through a growing period in his life. He was messing up in college; maybe in time he would learn.

I would use the experience I had acquired there some years later to get a job as an assistant manager at a store in Waukegan.

I thought about why David and I had married. In addition to both of us being so young, we were both anxious to leave home. I was living with my mother and grandmother, who had resented my close relationship with my mother.

David was the oldest of six children, and marriage gave him an excuse to leave a crowded house.

Another reason we married was because in 1964, that's what you did when you fell in love. You got married. Marriage was in.

David was born in Marion, Illinois. His mother and father lived in West Frankfort, Illinois. His father was 18 when he and Marie were already dating. He worked for the coalmines and would ride the coal cars out of the mine.

One day he was on the coal car when it jerked. He fell off and his leg was run over and severed. While in the hospital he became very depressed and thought no one would ever marry him with only one leg.

While still in the hospital, he asked Marie to marry him and was amazed when she said, "Yes".

After their marriage they bought a house for $5,000. It had a large stove for heat in the middle of the one-room house. It had no indoor plumbing.

David Edwin Largo was born on August 26, 1944, in Marion, Illinois. After David then came Diana, LaDonna, Richard, Ruth Ann, and Davey, who was adopted.

The family had moved to Chicago. David's father had moved up first and had got a job and found a place for them to live.

I lived right around the block from their house. Diana and LaDonna were a little younger than I, but we went to the same school and shared many of the same friends.

The first time I was in their home, one of the girls went into their parents' bedroom, and I walked in behind her. There stood a leg with a sock and a shoe on it. I gasped. She laughed. "Oh, that's my dad's leg. He's only got one leg." She said it as if it were nothing.

Marie worked as a waitress for King Burger on the corner of Milwaukee and Diversey Ave. in Chicago. Mr. Largo was working as a tool-and-die maker.

We ran with a good group of kids. We would ride our bikes; play baseball in the parking lot next door to our apartment. Before it was a parking lot, it had been a big Victorian mansion with a coach house in back. The city came in and tore the house down. Invariably the Chicago Police Department would chase us out of the lot.

There were about 12 of us in our group: six guys and six girls, all clean-cut kids. I still remember their names: the boys were Dennis, Paul, Kenny, Lance, Larry, and David. The girls were Karen, Nancy, Diane, Ladonna, Nancy, and Kathy.

Lance would have a pizza party at his house. His mother was Italian and made delicious pizza. We'd go to the Lane and Schurz High School socials. On a hot summer night, we'd hang out and ride to the park or go to the beach and go home for supper and get cleaned up and sit on one of the front porches and listen to a transistor radio.

David and I stayed married about eight years. In those eight years the military had him for six years and we had each other for two.

David died from cancer in Arizona while still married to Carol.

Chapter 6
Marrying Bob

Before leaving the bedroom, I sprayed myself with Chanel No. 5. I had on a pastel, pink suit, size 7, with a white, ruffled blouse. I was wearing three-inch heels and had a matching patent-leather bag. I wanted to look my best. After all, hadn't God chosen Bob for me?

Bob would be here any minute. Now my insides were jumping. We were going to catch a train at the Roselle Station and take it to downtown Chicago to the Courthouse and be married by a justice of the peace. I had never been to the Courthouse, and that added an element of excitement.

The door knocker sounded against the metal, and there stood Bob, just as he had the first day we had met. In fact, he was wearing the same outfit. I was disappointed that he hadn't worn a suit.

He was tall, slender, and good-looking. Under his brown hair were a pair of the gentlest blue eyes I think I had ever seen.

One thing about his face bothered me though. His lips. They were so large and full, as if they had been inflated with air. I thought, oh boy, they're big, but with all his other good features, I'll just have to learn to overlook this. I found out later that the large lips were from playing his trumpet.

After all, I wasn't perfect, but his compliments made me feel perfect. My mother had once told me, "With a little makeup, you'll be pretty." Now, what does that do to your self-esteem? It blows it out of the water. I would look in the mirror and think about what she said, and not feel very pretty.

We got on the train, and Bob and I talked for the whole hour it took to get to downtown Chicago. We were never short on conversation. The city didn't look as good from the train as it did from the highway. Things looked more rundown than I had remembered. I was born and raised in Chicago and knew the city well.

People downtown all seemed to be in a big hurry. The buildings towered over us, blocking the sun. With the chilly morning air, I was glad I had worn a suit.

We arrived at the Courthouse, and my insides were now turning cartwheels. It had marble floors and a lot of pre-cast moldings. The building looked old, and it felt cold -- not a cold *temperature,* but a cold that was lacking in warmth, in life. It had a high ceiling.

A police officer stood off to one side, while a short, old man with glasses was giving directions on where to go. He looked as old as the building itself, and perhaps he was. We asked him where the justice of the peace office was located.

"Get on that elevator over there and take it to the fifth floor," he mumbled, as if he had said it a million times.

The elevator looked and felt like a freight elevator. Bob's Old Spice cologne helped overpower the dirty, dusty smell. The slow elevator bounced to a halt, and we stepped into a hallway that was as drab and dusty as the one on the first floor.

We found a frosted glass window that would have said Justice of the Peace, had half the letters not been missing. The door rattled as we closed it behind us.

A lifeless-looking woman sitting at a desk asked us for our marriage license. She said, "Go stand over there," pointing to her left. I was glad to hear her say "stand," because I didn't want to sit and soil my pink suit touching anything.

The woman got up and opened the door into the justice of the peace office. This was a 10- by 10-foot office with a desk and a single window. I swear, the window hadn't been washed since the building had been erected in the early 1900s.

The justice was wearing a black robe, leaning back in a leather-backed chair. A cigar hung in the corner of his mouth. He rattled off some words that sounded to me like something coming from a robot. Bob and I both said, "I do."

He said, "Okay, you're married."

Leaving the room, we passed a waiting couple -- he was wearing a tux, and she had on a long, white gown. Five rainbow bridesmaids, five groomsmen, and both sets of fathers and mothers attended with her. I wondered how their big entourage could possibly squeeze into the JP's office. I further wondered how soiled the bride's white dress would get before she got out of this filthy Courthouse.

We got back onto the ancient, dirty elevator. When the doors closed, we kissed.

"I feel as though I just bought a pound of ground beef," Bob said. "I just couldn't get myself to kiss you back in that JP's room. I felt it would have been a waste."

Walking back to the train station, we stopped at a florist next door to the Greyhound Bus Station. Bob bought a dozen red roses. We had a few more blocks to walk to the train station and what seemed like a long wait for the train.

I was supposed to be working this morning but had asked Joyce, a co-worker, to fill in for me. When we got back, she told me, "Niame called. He's back from Syria." (Niame is pronounced Ni-EEM.)

Niame was a sweet, good-looking man who had moved from Syria to Chicago. I had dated him a few times and had even gone with him to his company's Christmas party. When he had asked me to go, he said he didn't know any beautiful women in the United States except for me. I had gone to the company party wearing a bright red organdy low-cut knit gown. I was a size 7, and after having two babies, I finally had a chest to be proud of. This dress showed every curve and had a ruffle collar that accented my well-formed breast. I had worn a wig that made me look like dynamite. He and his co-workers couldn't keep their eyes off me. I'm sure some of the wives at the party hated me, but I didn't care. We had fun.

On one date, he said he wanted to take me to a restaurant he had discovered in Morton Grove. We drove for about an hour, and I was sure this place was going to be special. When we pulled up, it was a fast-food restaurant that sold gyros.

During the drive home, he told me, "Jud-dee (that's how he pronounced Judy), I have never said 'I love you' to anyone, but when I do that, it will be to the woman I marry."

I was thinking that wouldn't be me. If you think I'll marry you just so you can remain in the United States, that isn't happening. Sorry, no green card. I may be blonde, but I'm not *that* blonde. I would never let those words roll off his lips. I talked about our differences and our religious difference so he'd get the picture clearly. He told me he was leaving for Syria and didn't know when he would return.

My roommate, Marie, had broken up with a young sailor and had gone home to Jacksonville, Florida. I had taken over her car payments, and now owned two cars. She didn't know if she would be coming back.

Chapter 7
Niame

Niame showed up the day I had married Bob, bearing a gift for my birthday that he had missed. It was a shoebox without a lid, with paper stapled over it. When I opened it, it was a *barometer!*

My first thought was, what is this? What am I going to do with it? Somehow I said, "Thank-you. You shouldn't have."

He was beaming. "I had looked around your office and knew you didn't have one." He was so sweet and would, no doubt, be good for the right woman. I just wasn't that right woman.

When Bob and I got back to the apartment after getting married, Niame called back. I broke the news to him that I had got married.

"Jud-dee, you are joking."

"No, it is no joke. It's real."

"I'm coming over," he said.

In five minutes he was at my front door. I introduced him to Bob, and that was when he had presented me with the birthday gift. When he left, he said, "You were divorced once before, and I will wait for you, Jud-dee."

It was Wednesday, my day off, and we were still living in the model apartment. Laundry was all around the living room, and dirty dishes were in the sink. Bob had just gotten home and was relaxing in a chair.

I heard a knock at the door. At first I thought about not opening it at all, but I finally went to the door and opened it about half way. A young couple was standing there. I said, "I'm sorry, we are closed, and I cannot show the model," and closed the door.

The knocking on the door started up again. I opened it and said, "I am closed and will reopen tomorrow."

The woman said, "I'm Carol."

I said, "I'm Judy. I'm really sorry," and I closed the door again.

The knocking on the door resumed. I opened the door again.

"I'm Carol, and he's John," the woman said.

Bob heard her and jumped up and said, "That's my brother. I had forgotten I had invited them for dinner,"

We took them out for pizza. I never did have a very good relationship with Carol and John after this. I guess my closing the door practically in their faces several times left a lasting impression that they just couldn't shake off.

Chapter 8
Getting Settled with Bob

That afternoon one of the owners of the apartment complex showed up and planted himself on the sofa in my office. I think this was how he got out of doing any work around his own house.

Sometimes he'd settle down in a big square rust-colored chair with arms that curled around the sides to the back. He'd sit in that chair and watch me handle potential renters. It made him feel like a king. He had even said that to me.

I had shared this with Bob, and when I showed him in that day, Bob headed right for that chair, forcing the owner to sit on the sofa. The sofa wasn't nearly as comfortable. Bob remained in the chair, prompting the man to leave much sooner than he ordinarily would. He'd talk money as though it were his and not his wife's. He was not very tall and had let himself go and was now rather portly. His clothes no longer fit very well.

Finally, 5 o'clock came around. I closed the office. Bob and I were finally alone.

"Is this what you go through every day?" Bob asked.

"Not quite this bad, but I am really busy every day."

A week later, Marie called. "I'm back," she said. "I'll be home in about an hour."

"Marie, why didn't you call me before you left Florida? You won't believe it, but I got married a week ago."

There was dead silence on the phone. I'm sure she was thinking where am I going to live?

"Come on over. I have a place for you. Bob has one more month on his old lease, and his furniture is still in the apartment. This will give you time to find a job."

In the meantime, a girl named Fran was looking for a roommate. Marie and Fran later moved in together. Bob and I then put his desk and bedroom set in storage for six months.

Our daily lives were being interrupted constantly. Bob couldn't take it, and said, "Let's start looking for a house."

So we did, and we bought a house that was about to be foreclosed.

Buying the house negated a contract at the apartment complex that would have given me title to the furniture in the model apartment. When I got the job as manager of the complex, I was given an apartment on the second floor, rent-free, immediately above the model apartment. But when a stranger would show up locked out of his/her apartment late at night, I would have to go down to the model, which was dark, and leave my boys unattended. This didn't sit well with me.

The demand for the apartments was high, in fact, there was a waiting list. I convinced the complex management company to let me move into the model apartment. They agreed, with the provision that the furniture would become mine after three years. I just had to buy furniture for the boys' bedroom that would match the colonial furniture in the rest of the apartment.

Chapter 9

The House from Hell

Here's how we happened to buy *the house from hell*.

I mentioned to a lady friend at my church that Bob and I were looking to buy a house. The woman told me of a little ranch-style house in Hanover Park that she had heard was going up for sale. Bob and I went to see it. We liked the location; it was next to a children's playground -- perfect for my two boys and for Bob's two boys.

What was this? The house was *pink*! It had *pink siding*!

The woman was blind, and her husband had gone to Boston to find a job. She had three children of her own at home and in addition, a young drug addict living with them.

The woman had a mother cat and kittens in the bathtub. There was a hole in the plastic tile so the cats could exit without passing the dogs tied to the front and back doors. Boxes of clothes were piled up along the inside walls.

The floor was covered with newspapers. Bob and I figured that the walls and floor were sound.

Bob looked at me and asked, "Why *this* house?"

"Because it's about to be foreclosed, and we can afford it," I said.

The woman told us, "Yes, I'll sell."

Then she said, "No, I won't sell."

"That's all right," I told her, "we'll find another house."

A few days later we got a call from our lawyer. He wanted Bob and me to come to his office at six o'clock. It was my son Richard's birthday.

We were surprised to see Joan, the blind owner of the ranch house, signing papers. He had us sit down.

"Mrs. Shechan's home is going to be foreclosed at midnight. If you are still interested in buying it, you'll need to do it before midnight."

Bob and I looked at each other. We really hadn't made a decision. We had looked at the house once very hurriedly. The price was right, and we wanted to get out of the apartment complex.

"What do we need in money?" Bob asked.

He rattled off some numbers. "Mrs. Shechan is three payments behind in her mortgage. At $125 a month, that's three monthly payments, totaling $375. In addition, there is a $5,000 lien on the property owed to a siding company. And there is $10,500 still owed on the mortgage."

Bob and I looked at each other again.

"You have only until midnight to sign the papers," the lawyer reminded us.

We signed. We were now homeowners.

A few days later Mrs. Shechan phoned us. She would really appreciate it, she said, if Bob and I would drive her to the airport. She was going to fly to Boston to be with her husband.

Bob was at work, so I asked my sister Joyce and my friend Nora if they would come with me to the house and help Mrs. Shechan and her children get packed so we could get her to the airport. I drove Nora in my car, and Joyce brought her car. Thank goodness we had two cars.

The three of us loaded seven suitcases, two trunks, two dogs, three kids, bags, a bag of treats to eat on the plane, a box of books and records for the blind, a violin, and, of course, Mrs. Shechan herself. Her 15-year-old was wearing an evening gown and a fur coat that one of the dogs had thrown up on en route to the airport.

Getting them to the checkout counter was a challenge. One of the dogs refused to get into a cage, but I was just as determined that it would get in. I won.

The trek down the corridor to the plane drew a lot of attention. Nora and I had all the records, and Joyce had the violin case and was pushing Mrs. Shechan toward the gate. Nora and I spotted one of those flatbed carts, the kind used by airport employees in hauling supplies around the airport. We borrowed it just long enough to get to the plane.

I'm sure the check-in clerks had never seen anything like this and more likely hadn't seen anything like it since.

We drove back to the house so Nora and Joyce could see our "new" dwelling place. Sandy, my sister-in-law, who was pregnant, also showed up for the tour. Five minutes after we started looking over the house, Sandy rushed to the front lawn and threw up.

"You're out of your mind," she said.

I agreed. Bob and I simply had not done our homework in inspecting the house before we signed on the dotted line. The place was *filthy*.

When Saturday came around, we were ready. We had arranged for a dumpster to be in the driveway for the debris we knew we would be hauling out of the house. *Seventeen* of our friends showed up to work, and work they did.

We literally *shoveled* junk out of the house and could not believe how quickly we filled up the dumpster. We phoned to have *another one* brought to the scene. Emptying out the attached garage quickly filled the second dumpster to overflowing. The garage had four washers and dryers, and trash literally to the ceiling.

So we phoned for *a third dumpster.*

But back to the house, the toilet was broken, and so was the bathroom sink. The door fell off the kitchen stove. The kitchen counter had a hole where the coffee pot had burned through.

Wheelbarrows full of trash from the back yard quickly filled dumpster number three.

Next, we discovered an attic filled with junk. We called for *dumpster number four.*

It was actually a small house, only 750 square feet, with three small bedrooms, a living room, an eat-in kitchen, and a bathroom.

Superwoman was still active. I had set a goal of two projects a day in addition to regular family chores. The projects included:

- Tear out bathroom walls
- Cut and log seven trees
- Wheelbarrow 8 yards of dirt and 8 yards of mulch
- Rip out the kitchen floor
- Wallpaper a room at a time.

Miracles really do happen. After 30 days of grueling hard work, which included a thorough cleaning and a fresh painting, we had actually made the house livable. Here's a list of some of the things we did.

We Installed new:

- Toilet
- Sink
- Carpet
- Bedroom doors
- Front door

We Replaced:

- Broken windows

- Major appliances

We moved in by Christmas.

Shortly thereafter, someone threw an ice ball through our garage window, striking our car. I phoned the police at noon to report the vandalism. A squad car didn't show up to investigate until 6 o'clock.

When we let the officer in, he exclaimed, "Oh, my God!" He said he deliberately kept putting off coming to the house. "I recognized the address. I just didn't want to come here. I'd been here a number of times. It was always too depressing."

The neighbors soon dropped by to thank us for bringing the property value back up.

We also made improvements to the yard. There had been seven trees in the back yard that had been planted too close together. Some were Russian olive and silver maples. I had watched a TV program on how to take down a tree and make it fall exactly where you wanted. It worked.

Back to that pink aluminum siding. We later learned that Mrs. Shechan's 12-year-old daughter had picked out the color. We soon found out that that color of siding had been discontinued 10 years ago. It didn't take us long to pay off the $5,000 lien on the siding and take ownership of the house free and clear.

We lived in the former *house from hell* for a year before we sold it for a tidy profit. I had made it my priority to do two or three projects a day in the house, which I did up to when we sold it.

We added white shutters, and I painted a thin gray line on them. We bought a white, cross-buck, self-storing storm door. We installed railroad ties around the base of the house for flower boxes. We brought in eight yards of dirt to level out the back yard. We planted grass and kept it mowed and planted lots of flowers. We painted the garage an ultra white. I painted gray trim around each of the 12 squares on the door.

We had turned the neighborhood eyesore into a beautiful ranch home.

The house sold two weeks after we put it on the market. Someone had told me the house would sell quicker if before a prospective buyer came, I would pop some homemade bread or an apple pie in the oven to give off an irresistible scent of home. It worked.

Chapter 10

A Perfect Storm on the Horizon

The week we were scheduled to close on the sale of the little pink house, trouble headed my way -- big-time. Little did I know it at the time, but it was the *perfect storm* in the making.

We were in the process of buying a bigger house in Hanover Park eight blocks away. It was only five houses from the school my boys would attend. We were going to invest the sale money from the pink house into the *new* house.

It had snowed all night and it was bitterly cold. Bob had gotten up at 5 o'clock to go to work. I was still sleeping when he woke me and said the car was stuck in a snow-bank in the driveway. Would I please help him free the car so he could leave and not be late for work? His company was about 17 miles away, and he had never been late or missed a day's work.

I put on sweatpants, boots, and a coat and helped dig the snow away from his tires. Bob's efforts to drive the car out failed, and I found myself pushing against the front of the car. The wheels spun, and I pushed; they spun some more, and I pushed, and I pushed, and I pushed. Finally the car was free, and Bob was on his way.

Back inside the house, I took off the sweatpants, boots, and coat and went back to bed. It took a long time to get warm again; I was chilled to the bone.

Seven-thirty rolled around, and I had to get up to get Richard off to school. Jacob was staying at his Grandma Largo's house (my first husband's mother).

My chest was hurting, and I thought it would just pass. I sent Richard off to school with his lunch, which was allowed on very cold, inclement-weather days. We lived eight blocks from school.

I went back to bed. By this time my chest felt as though someone had stacked gray cement blocks on it -- three high. I wanted to cry but I thought, no, if I cried, it might make things worse.

It seemed like a big problem, and it kept getting bigger.

"Oh, God, maybe I'm having a heart attack."

I prayed. "Lord, please help me."

I phoned Sandy; we had been close friends for years, and I knew I could count on her.

She had given birth to Karen, her third child, less than a month earlier, and she quickly showed up -- with the baby.

"Why don't you just call an ambulance, Jude?"

Then she said, "No, I'll call it for you."

I quickly phoned Bob and told him I was going to the hospital.

"I'll meet you there and don't worry, Honey," he said.

Bob arrived at Alexian Brothers Medical Center in Elk Grove, Illinois, before I did.

The emergency room took me in immediately. They took X-rays, gave me an EKG, and told me I was fine, that it was only anxiety.

"But I don't have anxiety." I said. Surely I was in denial.

They said I needed to make an appointment with my own doctor and get checked out thoroughly.

Bob drove me home, and I phoned a local doctor. When I told him I still felt a heavy weight on my chest, he took me in right away. His solution to my problem: a prescription for Valium. I was to take three of the pills a day. I was given 180 pills, enough for two months! I thought if I had wanted to do myself in, this was the perfect setup.

This was the week we were planning to move into our other house. My family members and my friends told me I was in no condition to be packing and moving, that they would do it for me.

It was just as well. The pills were making me feel like a zombie. And when I looked in the mirror, I thought I looked like a zombie.

They went ahead and moved us. When I woke up the next morning, I looked around, thinking this was heaven. The rooms were so much bigger; the house was so much prettier, and it all looked brand new to me.

Without the Valium, I would have been heavily involved in the moving, making sure everything was put exactly in its place.

Weeks went by, and I was a mess. Superwoman wasn't able to do it all. I had never been on this type of pill, especially three a day. I was an emotional basket case. I stood looking at the closet in our bedroom, picturing myself sitting on a shelf pulling the doors closed behind me.

While I was in this *fog,* I wondered: What had happened to my period? It was gone. I knew I wasn't pregnant. But my menstrual cycle had not come for several months. I knew this wasn't normal. Although I had had problems with period irregularity as a teenager, in recent years I had been very regular.

I phoned for an appointment with my OB-GYN doctor. He was really a nice person, and I knew I could trust him.

He took one look at me and said, "What happened to you?"

I guess it looked as though a truck had hit me. I showed him the pills.

"I don't need a crutch, I need help," I said. "I feel like I'm losing my mind."

He put me in the hospital and said, "We'll get to the bottom of this."

They ran every test they could think of. I was put in a room with a little old lady who was dying. She had a way of sleeping during the day and staying awake at night. When she would finally go to sleep, she would have a nightmare about fires. I'd gently touch her arm and rub it and call her by name in a calm voice and tell her the fire was out, she was all right, and she was in a hospital. I'd tell her the names of those who had come to see her while she was asleep. She told me I was an angel. I said, "No, I'm just your roommate."

They moved me down the hall the very next morning. She died at around noon.

My doctor came in with my test results at 8:30 that evening. He looked exhausted.

"The EKG shows there's been some scarring. But the other tests don't show anything." He told me to stop taking the Valium.

Regarding my not having had a period in the last few months, he said, "Women in concentration camps and prisons often don't have periods either."

He recommended I see a shrink, and he recommended a Dr. Spear in Chicago, whom he said he knew to be very good. He gave me his number and told me to make an appointment.

I left early on the day of the appointment so I could have plenty of time to park and get to his office on time. I was very apprehensive.

When I had shared with my sister Joyce that I was going to see a psychiatrist, she said, "I hope it's a good Christian doctor."

I said, "No, I don't know if he's a Christian or not, but I really don't care. I don't care if he's purple, as long as he can help me. He comes highly recommended and is supposedly one of the best."

I got to his office 15 minutes early. The secretary told me to have a seat. I sat down and just shook. A door slowly opened in an inner office, and a man stood in the doorway and motioned me to come in. My nerves took over, and I missed what he said as I walked past him. I think he introduced himself, but I just didn't hear it.

I sat down in front of his desk, and he took a seat behind it. Then I poured out all of the things that were troubling me -- to this complete stranger. I had been burying so many things in my emotions -- secrets that had been overwhelming in my mind.

When the session was over he said, "This session is free. Can I book you for next week?" I said Yes, and he handed me his card. I looked down on it and read the name of Dr. Green.

Whatever happened to Dr. Spear? Why hadn't someone told me that this wasn't Dr. Spear? It really upset me. Yet, I didn't say a word. I just left, knowing I had spent an hour with Dr. Green, whom I didn't know anything about.

The next week I went back. Dr. Green said, "Well, how are you doing? What would you like to talk about today? Do you have any questions?"

I said, "Yes. When I had made the appointment, I was told I would be seeing Dr. Spear. But when I got here, no one told me that it had been changed, nor had I asked for a change."

He apologized and said he would look into it to see what had happened.

"Your name simply came up on my chart," he said.

But I liked Dr. Green, and went to him for the next eight weeks. I would cry all the way home. No more pills, no more periods. But it was coming back, and I knew it would return, because *Superwoman* doesn't live here anymore.

I found out that I was as weak as I was strong. As I reflect back at all that had happened in my life, yes, I had locked myself up in a prison. Not a prison with bars. Not a prison building. It was just the way I had been dealing with unfortunate events or with tragedies in my life. And the Lord knows there had been a lot.

Yes, my period came back.

I was now 30 years old; Bob, 31; Rich, 10; Jacob, 6; and Bob's sons, Robbie and Rusty, the same ages as my boys. Bob was still getting custody on weekends.

My mother was working in downtown Chicago for some doctors and taking care of her mother and sister.

My father had remarried and lived in Wisconsin. We rarely ever heard from him.

Bob's parents were living in Twin Lakes, Wisconsin. He had retired as a Chicago policeman. Mrs. Neumann was into gardening, but Mr. Neumann was a couch potato.

I had been neglecting what once had been a very important part of my life -- God and my Christian faith.

My relationship with Bob began to change. While being kept busy in the *house from hell,* we didn't have time to notice.

The house we had bought only eight blocks away and only five houses from the neighborhood school had been owned by the secretary at the real estate office.

We made $30,000 profit on the *house from hell*. We put that money down towards purchase of that next house. It was two stories, white, with black shutters. It had an aboveground pool and a great back yard -- flowers, flowers everywhere.

Chapter 11
Contributing Factors

Other events ganged up on me to help create that *perfect storm.* It was 1979. In January the Chicago metropolitan area was getting *the big snow.* Snow was piling up deep at intersections, blocking visibility. Flat roofs on businesses and poorly pitched gabled roofs on homes were collapsing. People were getting up on their roofs to push off the snow.

Bob and I were living in the "big" house we had moved into after selling the pink house. When spring came, it rained for 16 days in a row, flooding our house. The pool collapsed sending 13,000 gallons of water onto the neighbor's backyard garden.

The parking lot at Bob's company flooded up to the doors. He phoned me at home and I told him, "Why not put our van up on shipping skids?" He did, and the van was saved.

The floodwaters were rising up to the floor of the house. The boys helped me remove the new carpet we had just put in the week before.

We were paying bills for *our* house and for *Bob's parents'* house in Twin Lakes, Wisconsin. The market had dropped, and we couldn't sell that house.

Bob's parents were ill, and we were trying to maintain their property. I was mowing the lawn on their large property. I was driving back and forth to Wisconsin to take care of them.

I was taking my mother to Maywood so she could visit her mother.

My boys were in sports. I was driving them around.

Carpenter ants ate the back porch. Bob had been tearing the downstairs of our house apart for a year.

Bob's dad died in Burlington Hospital, Burlington, Wisconsin, during the big snow of January 4, 1979. His aunt died in July, and my dad died in November of 1979.

Bob's mother, Mrs. Helen Neumann, had lived in Twin Lakes, Wisconsin, with her retired Chicago policeman husband, Bob Neumann Sr., whose sister, Adele Larson, had been living in Twin Lakes when Bob's father retired. When Adele offered to loan him a down payment for a house in Twin Lakes, he accepted her offer.

Adele was quite the controller. She had bought the houses on both sides of her home so she could control who lived there. She was out to impress the town.

Adolph Neumann, father of Bob Neumann Sr. and Adele, was living in a Twin Lakes nursing home. I think that's why she wanted her brother in Twin Lakes -- to help with their father's care.

Adolph was a handful. He would sneak out of the nursing home on many afternoons and go to the local tavern for a couple of beers. He would run a tab and tell the bartender to call his daughter, Adele, that she has money and would pay the tab. Besides, she would give him a ride back to the nursing home.

My Bob's parents, Bob Sr. and Helen, bought a house in Twin Lakes that had a living room, kitchen, bath, two bedrooms, and enclosed front and back porches. The lot was large -- well over half an acre.

Helen was Swedish and loved having company and preparing large meals. They were the best meals ever.

She had planted a garden and grew everything under the sun. She did canning and freezing.

Bob (my husband), after his divorce from his first wife, would take his two boys to Twin Lakes to spend weekends with Grandma and Grandpa. She would spoil the boys rotten. She had set up their second bedroom for the boys and would always prepare their favorite meals.

After depositing the boys with their grandparents, Bob would get busy mowing the half acre, repairing the bathroom floor, fixing the plumbing, painting, hanging wall paper, and fixing whatever else needed repairs.

Now and then a repair project would prove costly. One time he was chopping down a tree and put the ax through his foot, narrowly missing the bones.

Bob's father was quiet and content with watching TV. He always seemed to be wearing his green khaki pants. He had emphysema and had trouble breathing.

Bob was teaching his boys to ski at a nearby resort and was teaching Robbie to play the trumpet.

This is when I met Bob. He had told me early on that his mother would talk his arm and leg off while his dad sat and watched TV. But as it turned out, the opposite was true.

Bob's father and I hit it off right away. I, of course, remembered him as the policeman crossing guard at Delano School in Chicago. And, as it turned out, we knew many of the same people, all policemen.

Also, in the 1940s after World War II, Chicago's mayor was going to build up a police force like no other. After all, the military had trained most of the policemen. Some of our Chicago neighbors back then were policemen, and he knew them.

Bob's mother, meanwhile, was leery of me because I reminded her of Bob's first wife, who had hurt Bob badly. His mother didn't want to see him hurt again. But as she got to know me, after lots of dinners, painting, wall papering, and mowing the lawn, she warmed up to me and gradually became very talkative.

One day, Bob's father phoned us and said he had found his wife on the bathroom floor twitching and unable to speak. He said he had taken her to Burlington Hospital in nearby Burlington, Wisconsin. She had suffered a stroke.

It was horrible to see her like that. She responded to therapy and was able to speak again but she lost the use of her left side. Then she was moved to the home where her father-in-law had once lived. It made me sick. I would cry all the way home.

Her husband would be there to feed her every meal. The beds were so close together; you could reach out and touch someone.

The fact that with her right hand she could feel her numb left arm and that the woman in the bed next to her had such a deep voice prompted Helen to believe she had a man for a roommate. We tried without success to explain to her what was happening.

She fell out of bed when her husband wasn't there and no one reported it. Unbeknownst to the nursing home staff, she had broken her hip. She had complained of pain and discomfort, but no one had listened to her.

Finally, her husband asked the doctor to have her hip X-rayed. He did, and it was discovered that it was broken but that it had already started to mend. To repair it, they would have to break it again. Since she would never walk again anyway, they decided to let it mend on its own.

Before we found out about the broken hip, I had had enough of her nursing home. I called a meeting of Bob's father, Bob, Bob's brother John, and his wife, Carol. I was adamant that she needed to be placed in a different nursing home.

Bob's father spoke to her doctor, and soon he got her placed in a nursing home in Kenosha, Wisconsin.

On a Christmas day we were all at the Kenosha nursing home. We were elated. It was clean, with only two people to a room. The staff greeted everyone by name and did not ignore their needs. The food was served in a dining room with everyone present. The food looked good and she loved it. All I could say was "Thank you, Lord. Thank-you for the greatest Christmas gift any family could ever have."

One bad thing about having his wife moved to Kenosha, this meant about a 40-minute ride for him to get to the nursing home. Meanwhile, after about two years of dealing with his wife's stroke, *his* health was failing. He was going in and out of the hospital in Burlington.

I called him and said I wanted him to come to Hanover Park and move in with Bob and me. He said yes.

I had been praying to the Lord about him and Bob's mother for a long time. When he was admitted to the hospital, I went there one day. I remember the date. It was January 3, 1979. I asked him outright if he knew the Lord. I didn't want him to die and not go to heaven because I had been afraid to talk with him about the Lord Jesus Christ.

He said of course he knew the Lord. "What do you think has gotten me through all this?"

My heart leaped with joy. This had been a subject I could never bring up with my own father.

That's when I suggested to Bob's father that he move in with Bob and me.

When he said yes, I was flying. But he made me promise that if anything ever happened to him, we were to take the TV in the bedroom and give it to Adele.

Ironically the very next day the hospital called and said we needed to come quickly, that he had taken a turn for the worse.

It was snowing. I called Bob at work, and he was on his way. I called Carol and John, who lived about 45 miles south of us, and they were on their way.

I prayed, "Please, Lord, give us five minutes to tell him we love him; don't let him die before we get there."

We arrived at 3 o'clock. Five minutes later he died. Adele was sitting at his bedside. But Carol and John got there half an hour later.

I had hung my coat in the closet next to his pants, which had the keys to the house. Adele said to Bob and me, "I suppose you'll be selling the house. I loaned your mom and dad $15,000 when they bought the house."

Bob was shaken and told her we would discuss that later.

I remembered Bob's father telling us to return the TV to Adele. As we lifted the TV, there was a book, a bookkeepers' book showing every dime Bob's father and his wife had ever spent since living at Twin Lakes, along with a letter from Adele stating that the loan had been paid in full several years earlier. Bob's father knew -- he knew what we would be up against.

The services took place at Twin Lakes in the funeral home up the hill from Bob's father's back yard. In fact, the two properties abutted each other.

We had Helen brought to the funeral in an ambulance. We weren't sure she would understand that her husband had died. We had the doctor there when we told her.

"My Bob?" she said.

"Yes, Mom, your Bob," I said.

"Why, he told me we would go together in a silver casket," she said.

"I know, Mom," I said. "We talked with the undertaker, and he is going to arrange it if that's what you want."

We had instructed the funeral home to hold his ashes until Helen died. Three years later when Helen died, they were, indeed, buried together in a silver casket in Twin Lakes Cemetery.

You would have thought it was a party. She was so glad to see her neighbors and her sisters. For some strange reason, she didn't recognize her son John and his wife, Carol. She asked John, "And, who are you?" "I tried to tell him smoking would kill him," Helen said. "He just wouldn't listen." Then she would tell everyone within earshot, "Don't smoke!"

Bob's two sons and my two sons were at the service. We didn't know how the boys would handle their grandfather's funeral, since they had been close to him. He would often give each of them a quarter to go for ice cream at the corner of his street.

The boys were hesitant to go near the casket. Finally, Bob and I walked up to the casket with them. The heads of the younger boys, Rusty and Jacob, just cleared the edge of the casket.

"Nice suit," Rusty said. He had never seen his grandfather wear anything but green pants and a thermal knit shirt. Bob and I giggled.

The boys ran off to the funeral home coffee shop to have a good cry. We tried to comfort each one.

About an hour later, each of the four boys asked if they could have a quarter. We thought maybe they wanted to go for ice cream, since they knew the neighborhood. It wasn't until years later that the boys shared with us why they had wanted the quarters. When no one was looking, they went up to the casket and put all four quarters in their grandfather's pocket to take to heaven for ice cream.

Robert E. Neumann Sr. was born March 3, 1909, and died January 4, 1979. Services were held at Elm Lawn Chapel, Elmhurst, Illinois, January 8, with Rev. Kenneth Jensen, officiating. Six years later his body was moved to Twin Lakes to be buried in the silver casket as he had promised her (Mrs. Neumann). The funeral was conducted by Haase Funeral Chapel, Twin Lakes, Wisconsin.

The following obituary appeared in the Beloit Daily News, Beloit, Wisconsin, January 6, 1979:

Robert Neumann, 69

Twin Lakes -- Robert E. Neumann Sr., 69, of 559 Gatewood Ave., Twin Lakes, died on Thursday afternoon in Burlington Memorial Hospital after a long illness.

He was born on March 3, 1909, in Chicago, the son of Adolph and Augusta Neumann. He married Helen Matson on Aug. 2, 1940, in Elmhurst, Ill. He retired in 1972 from the Chicago Police Department, after having been employed there for 30 years.

He served in the U.S. Army as a medic during World War II in the European Theater. He was a member of the VFW, the American Legion, the Illinois Policeman's Association, and the Loyal Order of the Moose.

Survivors include his wife, Helen; two sons, Robert Jr. of Hanover Park, Ill. and John of Berwyn, Ill., five grandchildren; and one sister, Mrs. Adele (John) Larson of Twin Lakes.

Funeral services will be held at 11 a.m. Monday in the Elm Lawn Cemetery Chapel, Elmhurst, Ill., with the Rev. Kenneth Jensen officiating. Cremation will follow. Friends may call at the Haase Funeral Chapel in Twin Lakes from 2-6 p.m. Sunday and after 9:30 a.m. Monday at the cemetery chapel. In lieu of flowers, memorials may be given to the Twin Lakes Rescue Squad.

Some time after the funeral, as I watched the snow fall and cover my fresh footprints, I thought about Bob's father. I truly loved him; he was the father I had never had. He loved me, too. I wrote the following:

Footsteps

The footsteps in the snow
Are covered over with a blanket
As if they were never there.
Like old age coming upon
The bent old man,

> His life fades into years,
> And when he is gone,
> Was he ever there?
> Our memories buried
> With blankets of burdens.

After Bob's father's funeral, I sent a thank-you card to Adele for the beautiful flowers and enclosed a copy of the pay-off letter about the loan that Adele had written to Bob's parents.

With Bob's parents gone, now we had two houses to maintain. The market had dropped, and their Twin Lakes house just wouldn't sell.

I would go to Wisconsin twice a week, either to shovel snow on Wednesday or to mow the grass on weekends. We were still taking the boys along with us. With only a single income, it wasn't easy to keep both our house and the Twin Lakes house in repair.

After about a year and a half, a woman in her eighties who didn't want to live with her daughter but didn't mind if she was across the street, bought it.

Adele had planned and had paid for her own funeral. She died in 1988. She had picked out the dress, jewelry, and casket. She had paid for the dinner and open bar at a local restaurant. She even had a lady show up at the gravesite with her dog; all groomed, and place the dog's bows on the casket. She had talked to the priest and had paid for the limo for John and Carol.

Bob and I were amused when we read the inscription that Adele had put on her tombstone. The year of her birth was wrong, making her two years younger.

Later Bob and I were in shock when we learned that we had been included in her will. Her estate was divided five ways: John (Bob's brother) and his wife, Carol; Bob and me; and a woman back east whom we did not know.

Bob and I rarely saw Adele. I guess we were too much like her brother in that we couldn't be bought.

After Adele's death, Bob and I took a cruise to the Caribbean and bought a van. We badly needed a vacation. Our lives had been in constant turmoil. It was time for a rest. We were finally free.

One day while Bob and I were visiting his mother at the Kenosha nursing home, I asked her, "Mom, if you could do anything in the world, what would you want to do?" She had two sisters and a friend who would often visit her. Her sister Elsie was very ill with cancer.

"I'd really like to see Elsie again before she dies," she said.

"Mom, I think we can probably make that happen."

Later I called her sister Irene, who lived with Gerry, a friend. They said Elsie was staying with them along with Elsie's daughter Sandy, who had come from California to be with her mother. Sandy was a nurse. They invited us to bring Bob's mother over for the visit.

I phoned four days ahead of time for an ambulance to pick up Bob's mother. The money was in her account, and if she didn't use it, the government would take it. When the ambulance arrived, it frightened the neighbors. They thought Elsie had died.

It was a great reunion for the sisters. Helen said I had lied when I told Elsie she looked great. She was correct; Elsie had indeed looked awful.

I told Bob the next evening when he came home from work that we needed to go to the hospital right away. He said he was too tired and wanted to wait until the next day. I said tomorrow could be too late; we had better go now to visit Elsie.

We got to the hospital at seven o'clock. By nine o'clock, she was dead. It was in early July.

A few months later Bob and I and my two sons were at Irene and Gerry's home for Thanksgiving dinner. We hadn't seen them since Elsie's funeral. The boys always enjoyed going there because the two ladies loved to have fun. They had been world travelers; neither one had ever married. They weren't *old maids;* they were simply *hidden treasures.*

The heat in the kitchen was overwhelming. Candles were burning across the big dining room table and on the buffet near where I was sitting.

Dinner was about to be served, and the wine and before-dinner drinks were hitting me bad. I excused myself from the table and went to the bathroom. I started removing my suit -- one piece at a time. I thought I was going to pass out. First the jacket, then the blouse, all the way down to my pants and bra. I wet a washcloth with cold water to cool me down.

Time was going by, and I kept hoping that nobody had noticed my absence from the table. I succeeded in cooling myself down and not passing out. I got dressed and went back downstairs to dinner. I simply explained that I was overheated and had to cool myself down a bit.

Helen Virginia Neumann

Bob's mother lived for six more years. Helen Virginia Neumann was born April 16, 1908, and died December 25, 1985. Services were held at Haase Funeral Home, Genoa City, Wisconsin, Saturday, December 28, 1985, Rev. Vincent Leach, officiating. Burial was in Mound Prairie Cemetery, Twin Lakes, Wisconsin. Haase Funeral Home conducted the funeral.

Chapter 12

A Look Back

This might be a good time to reflect on my childhood.

My father, Alfred (Al) Raymond Smith, was born in Missouri in June of 1914, and died in Oshkosh, Wisconsin, in November of 1979, my son Richard's birthday.

My mother, Bonnagene (Bonnie) Faye Steel Smith, was born in Missouri in May of 1917. She died in February of 2005.

My parents had four children:

Alfred (Al) Raymond Smith Jr., was born in August of 1936. He was a first-year wedding anniversary gift to Mom and Dad.

Ward Lee Smith was born in October of 1938.

Joyce Ann Smith was born in October of 1940.

World War II broke out, so there was a delay in the two-year plan. Dad served in the Navy and was stationed at Pearl Harbor after the bombing.

Superwoman doesn't live here anymore

I (Judith (Judy) Faye Smith) showed up in February of 1946.

As a little girl, I remember our family living in a basement apartment in Chicago. The rent was only $25 a month, but then it was increased to $35. It had one bedroom, a living room, dining room, kitchen, and you had to walk through the basement past the furnace and coal bin to get to the bathroom. The landlord didn't want to spend a dime on the building, but was sure willing to accept free labor from my dad. For a long time we didn't have a lawn, until we planted it ourselves.

Mother was a *clean freak* in those days. She had come to know the Lord as her personal savior, and had heard that "Cleanliness is next to godliness." We had an old wringer washer, which sounded to me like it went *wishy-washy-wishy-washy.* Mom would wring the clothes out into the bathtub to rinse and then wring them out again. She would hang them outside in summer, and in the very large bathroom in the winter. The bathroom had a tub at one end, a toilet at the other end, and a sink in between.

It was not a common practice back then to take a bath daily. You would bathe on Saturday and wash at the sink the rest of the week. After our Saturday night baths, we would sit on the linoleum in the living room and listen to the radio. That is, until 1951, when we got a 19-inch TV, when we'd watch the fights. We would snack on Charlotte Freeze, an ice-milk treat.

Al was blond, Ward had dark hair, and Joyce and I both had *white* blond.

On Saturday mornings, instead of putting on play clothes, usually pants and shirt, Joyce and I would sometimes put on dresses. We would go out in front of our house and stand there leaning against our railing with our hands behind our backs looking very shy. We had some Hasidic Jewish men living in the neighborhood. They had long curls at the sides of their heads and wore long, black coats, black pants, and they had those yarmulkes, which we called beanies, on the backs of their heads. They almost looked like they were wearing clothes that were too big. On their way to the synagogue, they would pat our heads and say, "Look at those pretty little blondies." Then they would reach into their pockets and hand us each a nickel. We would be very grateful and say Thank you. The nickel was enough for us to buy a whole week's worth of penny candy at Hy's candy store two blocks away on Pulaski.

Years later I learned that "the man of my dreams," Bob, my second husband, had been inside Hy's drinking cherry Cokes or phosphates, a mostly foam drink made of chocolate, a spoon of ice cream, and seltzer water.

I still fondly cherish memories of Hy's. We would pass there every day on our way to school. It had a big, old soda fountain with a black and white floor. A lot of the woodwork was wine-colored. The chairs were stools pressed up against the soda fountain. Sometimes we would have enough money to order a chocolate, strawberry, or cherry phosphate, occasionally mixing the various flavors together.

All four of us went to Delano School on the west side of Chicago. Al and Ward had left this school and gone onto high school by the time I started.

We were living at 4118 Adams, two blocks west of Pulaski. Our crossing guard was a Chicago policeman who rode a three-wheel motorcycle. He lived at 4600 Adams. Unbeknownst to me at the time, 22 years later he would become my father-in-law. I would learn to love him dearly.

Big sister Joyce Ann used to walk me in my buggy. I think she thought I was okay until I got old enough and had to go with her to different activities. As I got older, and she had to take me to her girlfriend's house, then I was just a pest.

I used to roller skate up and down our block singing "The Old Rugged Cross." I think that's when I began to be a "holy roller." I would roller skate down to the Lutheran church at the end of our block on Saturdays and wait for the weddings. The brides would be out in their beautiful dresses.

Our neighborhood was mainly Irish and Jewish. It seemed like there were churches on every corner. Practically every yard had lots of flowers with freshly mowed lawns, and most back yards had clothes strung out on clotheslines.

A little Italian man pulling a cart would come around and give three or four children at a time a ride around the block for 5 cents. He was short and wore a blouse-type shirt with baggy pants, a vest, and a hat. A short, black mustache accented his weathered face.

Another Italian man played an accordion and had a dressed-up monkey. The man would place his hat on the sidewalk while he played songs, and the monkey would dance around the hat. The monkey would pick up the hat and pass it around to collect money.

Then there was the iceman who delivered ice for the wooden iceboxes, which were popular at the time. While he was making deliveries, we would grab chips of ice off the back of his truck and suck on them.

Another regular was the waffle man, who drove a truck that was wooden on the outside with glass windows all around. He would make fresh waffles. For a nickel you could buy two waffles covered with powdered sugar. For 15 cents you could get two waffles with some Neapolitan ice cream in the middle.

We also had an organ grinder and a Good Humor ice cream truck making regular rounds in the neighborhood.

After the war the City of Chicago was growing leaps and bounds, and the push was on for an increased presence of police in the neighborhoods. The father of my best friend, Diane Lightfoot, who lived six doors away, was a policeman.

Gangs soon were starting up in the neighborhood. I can remember the names of some of them: the Blackstone Rangers and the Taylor Street gangs.

Diane, who was nine, was Catholic and went to a different school. She lived in a house half way down the block -- in between the house that had had a fire on the second floor and a house where a little old lady named Sarah had lots of flowering plants and used to give me beautiful, colorful ribbons.

Sarah would come out and invite me in. She would give me colorful bows, and I would leave and get locked in the hallway at the front of her building. The door was too heavy for me to open.

One day at lunchtime when I was six, my mom was calling me, and I couldn't get that door open. No one knew I was in the hall. I opened the mail slot on the door and hollered to my mother that I was stuck inside the hall.

Diane lived with her mom and dad (the cop), her elderly Aunt Marian, who I think was an old maid, and her toddler twin brothers.

One day her mom asked Diane and me to stay with the twins while she ran to the store. The twins were asleep in their room; we were in the living room. We heard them stir, and Diane went into the kitchen to heat their bottles. I was going to hold one and feed him while she fed the other.

When I looked into their room, one was standing in his crib smearing petroleum jelly on the wallpapered walls.

I called to Diane, who came running, but had left a towel on the stove too close to the flame. When she went back into the kitchen to get the bottles, she jerked the burning towel into the sink and doused it with water. But by this time the house had filled with smoke. The baby bottles got too hot to serve, and the twins' beds were covered with petroleum jelly, as were the twins themselves, like greased pigs. We had called the fire department, which arrived at the same time as Diane's mom.

Whenever I think of Diane's aunt, I can always smell the aquamarine lotion she would often put on our hands.

One summer Diane's parents let us paint a storage area in the back of the basement. The color of the paint was baby blue. By the time we were through, Diane and I were baby blue along with the walls, ceiling, and floor.

Diane had an uncle who lived upstairs. He would play Irish music real loud. But what I remember most about him was the smell when he would wet the bed, and urine would drip down through the ceiling.

At school I had a friend named Vivian. Vivian's sister, Deanna, and my sister, Joyce, were friends. They were poor, and their mother drank heavily and slept during the day. Vivian and Deanna used to brag about all the high-heel shoes their mother owned. They would come home from school and put together a lunch consisting of an egg, Twinkies, and cup cakes. Their mother died at an early age, and her children went to live at Mooseheart in Aurora, which I'm sure, offered them an improved home life.

When Joyce and Deanna graduated from grammar school, they hadn't shared with each other what kind of dress they would wear to their graduation. Both showed up wearing identical dresses.

Mother made sure we children were brought up in the church. She brought us there every Sunday -- first for Sunday School and services, and then again in the evening for services. I loved the singing, and still remember many of the Bible stories.

My brother Al wanted to be a minister. He would have been a good one. When he graduated from high school, he was president of his class. He won a scholarship and went to Ottawa University in Ottawa, Kansas.

When Al and our brother, Ward, were growing up, they used to fight. Not to be mean, but just to see who was the stronger. To try to prevent Joyce from telling our parents, they would tie her up and put her in a closet and take her shoes. We were always told to wear shoes to prevent catching cold from the cold floors. They would give me a gumball, and I would watch but never say a word.

Al and Ward had paper routes, and Joyce would help them by going house-to-house selling subscriptions. They would earn points for new subscriptions, and would pool them to buy Christmas gifts for all of us. I remember Al and Ward getting a carom board, and Al getting a baseball game. Al would sit on the front steps with that game, and it sounded like a full baseball stadium. I don't remember what Joyce got, but they brought me a Wanda Walking Doll.

Mom and Dad bought me a blue buggy with baby blocks all over it to walk my doll. One day Billy, the brat down the block, threw an ice ball through the buggy's hood. Diane ran and caught him and beat him over the head with a child's snow shovel. Billy never bothered me after that.

Ward's vision was poor, and it seemed he was always getting hit by either cars or by the Salerno Butter Cookie truck. He went downtown to an eye doctor weekly.

When I was very young, Al and Ward thought it would be fun to get me to memorize the names of all of the books of the Bible. After I learned them, they told the pastor. One Sunday morning he called me to the front of the church and asked me to recite them. I did -- without any mistakes.

Mother would lead us in daily scripture reading and bedtime prayer. She taught Sunday School and was good at it. Before I started school, she would take me to Bible study during the week. I remember being served tea, coffee, and sweets, and playing with a small dog.

I used to tag along with big sister Joyce to the park or playground or to her friends' houses. She used to tell Mom, "Do I have to take the brat?" Fortunately our relationship improved, as we got older.

While we were growing up, there was this thing called *hand-me-downs.* Being the youngest of four children, I saw a lot of those. Mother would take all of us to a seamstress on Washington Street, who would have us try them on and then pin and sew until the clothes fit perfectly. No one ever knew they weren't new.

On Sunday afternoons we would gather all the chairs in the living room, and Dad would show movies. Mom would make popcorn, and we would invite our friend.

Dad was "Mister Fixit." It seemed there wasn't anything he couldn't make or fix. I used to love to watch him to see how things were made. He would always say his repairs were only temporary, never permanent.

After Dad came back from World War II, about the time I was born, he took up drinking, which gradually got worse and worse. He had come by it rightfully. His dad had been a heavy drinker and had died before I was born.

His mother was very overweight, had a hard time walking, and it was said that she died of sleeping sickness. I believe she was a diabetic and went into a diabetic coma.

Diabetes seemed to have gotten into our genes. Al and Joyce are both diabetics, and I am a borderline diabetic. Ward somehow is diabetes-free.

It was on Al's 16th birthday, I was 6, and I begged him to ride me on the cross bar of his bike. He did. I was wearing a white pinafore dress. Gram and Uncle Eddie were at our house for dinner to celebrate Al's birthday. Dad was out at the tavern celebrating their 17th anniversary. Al asked if I wanted to steer, and I steered us right into a car. I fell under it and cut my eyebrow on the running board. I was screaming and bleeding all the way home. On this, my first visit to a hospital, I required seven stitches. I remember that Al, feeling responsible, didn't come home till late that night. But the mishap wasn't his fault.

Gram, as I called my maternal grandmother, had moved up from Kansas City, Missouri, and she was working at a printing company. At that time her name was Mabel Viola Roberts Steel. Although she had her own problems, she was able to help Mom raise the children.

When my mom was 17, her father, after having just got paid one day, was on his way home from work, and someone beat him up and left him slumped over a car in an alley -- dead. He had been robbed.

His name was Lester Steel, and he worked in the printing business. He was good to his family and was well loved in the community. His funeral was one of the biggest Kansas City, Missouri, had ever seen.

Mom and Gram had been very close. Mom had run off to Chicago and got married to Daddy at the age of 18. She was married on August 3, and a year later to the day; on August 3 Alfred was born.

This left Gram to raise Aunt Joyce, who was 13 at the time. Aunt Phyllis was already married to Milt and was traveling with him on his job. Aunt Phyllis, my mother's older sister, was short with bright, red hair In their early years of marriage, they had moved a lot and had lived with relatives from time to time.

After Aunt Joyce was married to Don, Gram moved to Chicago and found a job as a proofreader, where she met and began dating Eddie Yokum. They started going to church together and soon were married. We had referred to him as Uncle Eddie before they were married because we wanted to be respectful. Gram's name then became Mabel Viola Roberts Steel Yokum. Eddie was tall and slender and really liked kids and just adored us. They lived in a small apartment about four blocks from us on Washington. He loved to cook and was very good at it.

They soon introduced Mom to the church, and then Mom got involved and got all of her children involved.

Gram and Eddie went to the same church, where he had turned his heart over to the Lord. But he could not conquer alcohol. A minister who had told him he would not go to heaven had misled him. One night in despair, he turned on the gas stove, made his nighttime sandwich, and went to bed, dying in his sleep.

I'm sure the minister who told him he wouldn't go to heaven had been wrong. I'm certain he *is* in heaven.

I remember going to his wake, crematory, and funeral home. His ashes are buried in Deer Park Cemetery on the south side of Chicago.

It was Gram who discovered the church where Mom used to take us children. It was a Baptist church, even though Gram had been raised in a *Mormon* household.

Back to Gram, at the time of her birth in 1896, her mother had had abscessed teeth. When Gram was born, there were boils all over her head and upper body, and her immediate family thought she wouldn't make it.

They packed her in cabbage leaves, which, they said, would suck out some of the poisons. Neighbors told them they were wasting their time that the baby wouldn't live much longer. Although she suffered from migraine headaches from an early age, she outsmarted them; she lived to 93.

Gram was child number seven in her family, and her mother died when Gram was only six months old. Abscessed teeth may have contributed to her death. Gram never knew her real mother. Her aunt and uncle, who lived on a farm, took her in because she was so young, even though they already had seven children of their own. Gram's brothers and sisters stayed with her father and were raised by him.

Gram's aunt and uncle were believers and prayed and laid hands on her. Gram used to love to tell me that she was the original cabbage-patch baby.

Gram had to quit school after the fourth grade and worked on a farm. But she took up working crossword puzzles and ended up with a large vocabulary. She took pride in being a well rounded proofreader.

I don't think anyone in our family ever looked down on Gram. Instead we always praised her for what she had accomplished. She not only supported herself, but she also helped her daughter Phyllis in a time of need.

As Gram grew older, she aged well, both in her thinking and in her appearance. She didn't like antiques or anything old. She had had a tough life but had weathered the storms pretty well. She wasn't bitter.

Her skin was smooth and blemish-free. Her hair became white at the top but remained dark brown at the nape of her neck. She dressed well, loved hats, and always smelled good. She looked 10 to 20 years younger than she was. And, she was very active.

She worked up to the age of 89, her last job in the gift shop at the retirement home. Her complexion was peaches and cream.

She dressed well; Mother knew her taste and would shop for her. She had her hair done weekly at the retirement home. Her posture was good, and she was well read, keeping up with current events and enjoying novels. She had a great sense of humor.

But Gram had one flaw. After she retired, she came to live with Mother and me. She became attached to Mother and put the taboo on any and all relationships Mother would ever have with men. I believe she was jealous of the relationship mother and I had.

But Gram still hurt inside sometimes. In my pre-teens, she would come over for Sunday dinner, lay her hat on the bed, then go sit in the kitchen and cry, telling Mother of the latest fight she had had with Phyllis. This was a weekly thing. In case you forgot who Phyllis is, she was Gram's daughter and Mother's sister.

Gram went in the hospital for headaches. When Gram left the hospital, she was put on insulin, and this meant shots. I had the hospital teach me how to administer her shots, even though I used to pass out at the thought of a needle. I prayed for the Lord to help me get used to it. It was a good thing Gram's hearing was almost gone, because every time I'd give her a shot, I'd grimace with an "Ouch."

Phyllis and her husband, Milt, were known for their loud arguments. Phyllis wouldn't back down, and Milt would try to out-shout her.

One Christmas Eve, Gram went to bed early with one of her headaches. At the time she had a broken arm from a fall she had taken. When she went to bed, Phyllis and Milt were fighting. When she woke up to the sound of Christmas songs from the living room, she thought she had died and gone to heaven. Then reality set in; it was the family singing.

Mother and I were at the retirement home the day before Gram died. Gram and Aunt Phyllis were both getting worse by the day, and we didn't know who would die first. Gram died while we were en route to the retirement home.

She had signed over her insurance policy to the home, and they would bury her. Or, so we thought.

When Mother and I got to the funeral home, we found out the truth. The funeral director had been paid to have a *direct burial:* no service, no wake, nothing.

Mother and I were shocked. This would never do. After all, Gram had a daughter near death and another daughter in California who would be coming in.

We asked the funeral director what it would cost if we used one of his caskets and put a doily on top, with an open Bible and a single rose, with flowers at both ends of the casket, long enough for us to have a morning service.

I think he charged us $175 for the room and the casket. Actually, they had gone ahead and buried Gram the day before. But it was our secret.

Gram had told us the Bible verses she wanted read and the songs she wanted sung. By doing this, it came to pass, and no one needed to know. It would have upset her other two daughters without a doubt.

We had a friend do the service, and an organist play the hymns Gram wanted, and another friend sing. We provided the lunch that followed.

We had even asked the funeral director not to fill in the date in the sign-in book until after the service so no one would notice what the date of burial actually was. Gram would have been proud.

Phyllis called Mother later and said she was on the way to Weiss Memorial Hospital in Chicago in an ambulance and asked for Mother to come. I picked up Mother, and we went. We had been there many times and knew our way around the hospital.

In the emergency room, the desk clerk said, "She's right over there." I pulled back the curtain, and there lay a lady with carrot-orange hair and a short, stocky body. But her face was twice the size of Aunt Phyllis. I said, "Phyllis?" The woman just looked at me like, Who are you? A voice from the other side of the curtain said, "Judy, is that you? I'm over here."

Thank God! I thought. I couldn't imagine what had happened to Phyllis to make her face that swollen. I was relieved when I saw Aunt Phyllis that nothing had happened to her face. I couldn't tell her there was another lady in the next bed with the same orange hair.

Phyllis was in and out of the hospital many times toward the end of her life. One time she asked me to drive her out to the cemetery on Irving Park Road, about 45 minutes from her house. Steve, her son, was going to go but at the last minute backed out. It was just the two of us. I was thinking I'd take her for ice cream afterward. She didn't get out much in those days.

When we were half way there, I checked her oxygen. It was not working right and was discharging too fast. She needed the oxygen, and I had to rush back to her apartment. I drove like a maniac. We pulled into the driveway, I asked a man to hold the door. He in turn told his daughter to hold the elevator.

I popped the trunk, got her wheelchair out, and her in it, and rushed her through the hall to the elevator. I unlocked her door and turned on the oxygen and gave it to her and dropped in a chair exhausted. I swear, that day cost me 10 years off my life.

Mother and I met with her caseworker and were told all she would need before she could enter a nursing home. Mother and I had shopped and finally found one that would meet her needs. Just when we thought we had one selected, Phyllis would always find something wrong with it.

I had spent the weekend on her uncomfortable sofa working on all her nursing home requirements. When Mother and I would leave Phyllis's apartment, we would always feel drained.

Phyllis was a drama queen and a real manipulator. I had allowed it, but I had my fill. I cried most of that night and sat and wrote Betty, her daughter in New York, and Gary, her son in Kentucky.

It wasn't long before Phyllis died. Betty came in the week before, and Betty and I went to her doctor's office. Phyllis's breathing had been severely impaired from years and years of smoking. But we didn't tell her doctor. He wondered how could she have such terrible lungs if she hadn't been a smoker? Betty and I knew she had smoked like a chimney, lighting one off the end of the other practically all day.

Mother and I stayed overnight at the hospital. One of the technicians had failed to reconnect her oxygen, and Phyllis was removing the oxygen mask to breathe. I called for a nurse, who then accused me of disconnecting it.

Mother and I went down to the cafeteria for lunch and ran into her doctor. But when we got back to the room, Phyllis was dead. Her son Steve was at her apartment, and we called him. He was bi-polar and had been very close to Phyllis. We also phoned Betty and Gary.

Phyllis's roommate was a lady who was wearing bandages wrapped around her entire head. Her eyes were blackened and swollen. She looked as if someone had beaten her with a baseball bat. We asked the nurse what had happened, and she said it was a face-lift gone badly. Real bad. She had been transferred from another hospital. The poor woman almost died.

Once Mom got involved with a church, she got us four children involved. Each child had a youth group to go to. Mom became a Sunday school teacher, and because I was an infant, I went to the infant's area, but as I grew older, Mom was my Sunday school teacher.

Mom was very creative in ways to get children to learn their Bible verses. She built a little kitchen out of soapboxes and orange crates. Then she added a little living room and gradually added more rooms. As the children learned a Bible verse, they would advance to the next room.

Mom had some talent as an artist and was a good cook as well. She was especially skilled at stretching a dollar. She could make a meal and make it stretch for all of us. She made numerous potluck dinners for the church. She would always take enough for six people.

When I was six or seven, we moved to the north side of Chicago into a big two-story, white stucco house at 3709 N. Ridgeway. It was two blocks away from Aunt Phyllis's house. She had found both of the houses through a real estate office. The state had bought the houses with the idea of tearing them down in about two years to build the Kennedy Expressway. The rent was only $80 a month.

Mother had referred to the basement apartment where we had lived as "the cave" and the big house on Ridgeway as "the castle."

By this time I was attending James Murphy School. It was a long way from our house and involved a lot of walking.

There were eight windows on each side of the front door and an enclosed front porch. It had a large living room, dining room, and kitchen on the first floor. The second floor had two small bedrooms, a large bedroom, and a huge bathroom. It also had a full basement and a garage.

There were flowers in the front yard. The back yard had flowers in a bed five feet wide and about 50 feet long all the way from the house to the gate at the alley. We had flowers on the table all summer long.

Someone had taken great care of the house, and now it was our turn. It had hardwood flooring throughout. Two big stained-glass windows adorned the living room. Another large stained-glass window was at the top of the stairway.

Our next-door neighbors were *nudists*. The parents and their son and daughter would sit at the dining room table eating in the buff. We children would watch them through little squares in the stained-glass windows. Mother had no inkling that we were spying on them.

Mother had bought a beautiful used dining room set. We called it "the King Arthur" because it was so massive. It was wine-color with knobby legs with a lot of turnings. It included a china cabinet and a nice buffet. Now we had enough room to store everything.

Later on when we moved, Mom sold the dining room set for just $25. Some 35 years later I saw one just like it in an antique shop priced at $12,000. If only we had known.

Gram, my mother's mother, came up from Kansas City. Now that we had sufficient space for it, she brought her good china and crystal set and said, "Bonnie, I want you to have these." We put the precious china and crystal sets in our dining room set where they would be safe.

The dining room table, with all the leaves in it and all the chairs around it would seat 12 comfortably.

The kitchen was very large, what I would call a *country* kitchen. It had three walls, with two of them loaded with cabinets from the floor to the ceiling the length of the room. There were two windows off to the side where we put a table in front of it.

Dad used to make us breakfast, and he would cook bacon and eggs and put them on the table. The dog would leap up there and lap them up and run off. By the time Dad turned around with the next set of eggs and the next batch of bacon, he would finally realize that the dog was eating for all of us. Dad had picked him up off the street, figuring he was homeless and needed a home.

Gram moved in with Aunt Phyllis, my mother's older sister by 18 months. She and Uncle Milt had three children: Betty, Gary, and baby Steven. Their rented house was only two blocks away and also was to be torn down for the expressway.

Betty, who was a year younger than my sister, Joyce, was adorable, with real cute curls and reddish-blonde hair. She had been exposed to activities that my sister, brothers, and I never were. She took toe and tap dance and ballet and had all the costumes. She used to do backbends and twirl a baton, performing in parades. Later in life she had years of serous back problems.

Gary was four years younger than I was, and Steven, three years younger than Gary.

Phyllis's family did all kinds of things that we didn't do. That's because they had a car, and we didn't. Milt would take them out for picnics. We took public transportation now and then to downtown. We would take a bus or trolley to Madison Street to picnic in Grant Park and then go out on the lake in a Wendella boat. I remember on these excursions seeing some Amish people, who really stood out in a crowd.

When my family lived in the basement apartment, Phyllis and Milt lived in Portage Park. Betty went to Hayes School. By coincidence, years later she became Mrs. John Hayes.

I remember staying overnight at their apartment, in a brick three-flat building with a tree outside the bedroom where Betty slept. Betty, Joyce, and I used to stay up late making up scary stories while the tree was blowing in the wind. A street light behind the tree would cast eerie shadows on the wall.

I recall Phyllis having a tablecloth on the table for breakfast and a special glass jelly holder. We didn't have one. I had only seen jelly in jars.

Phyllis and Gram, along with Betty, Gary, and Steven, came to live with us when Steven was 18 months old. Mom would baby-sit Steven and Gary while Gram and Phyllis worked. With so many people in our house, the walls really rocked. But it was fun.

Phyllis finally had to leave Milt as his sickness grew worse. The police would pick up Milt, who would then talk his way out of their custody, saying Phyllis was going through the change.

Alfred was in college, Ward had gone into the Air Force, and they were having a difficult time. Milt was sick and was in and out of hospitals. Mother had offered to let them stay with us. Dad agreed and so we opened the doors and they came: Phyllis and Gram, Betty, Gary, and Steven. Mother would baby-sit Steven, make lunches for everyone, and get us off to school or work, whatever it took.

Other memories of "the old neighborhood" pop up from time to time. Here are some of them:

There was a neighbor down the block who had lost his legs in a motorcycle accident. He wasn't nice, and when his dog gave birth to pups, he tried to drown them in the sewer. It didn't work. Some neighbors saw him and saved them.

When I was eight, another neighbor down the block, a brand new father, invited all the neighborhood kids into his house to see his baby daughter. She was beautiful in a bassinet that looked like the one in "The Lady and the Tramp" movie.

You never stop to think about what influences your life. When I was pregnant with Richard, the bassinet was fashioned after one that had impressed me years earlier.

I remember the neighbor in that old neighborhood who built a boat in his back yard for Lake Michigan. He hadn't thought ahead, and after it was done, it was too large to get it out of his yard.

Then there was the man across the alley that bred bulldogs and boxers.

Next door was Vito, who one time started a fire in a 55-gallon drum and threw in a dog, killing it. I stayed as far away from him as I could. His grandmother was a bit off the wall. She would dump water over the third-floor banister down into our yard while we children were playing. I guess we bugged her.

One time we children tried to build a fire under our back porch for a camp-out to cook some potatoes. We got caught.

Then there was the lady across the street. Mom baby-sat her daughter a few times. Her name was Cratcha. We called her Cratcha Boonya.

A little girl down the block used to wear halter-tops, but they were always down. We used to tell her to pull the halter up and cover her dots. Sometimes when we saw her mom, *her* dots weren't covered either. The mother came down with TB.

Back at our house, we would play Ted Mack's Amateur Hour. Each of us would get up and do a comedy act, sing, or pantomime a record, such as "Mrs. O'Malley's Cat Came Back," "Grandma's Lye Soap," and "Home, Home on the Range."

Later in life I heard that *tragedy plus time equals humor.* Any one of us could have been a comedian.

In the meantime, Joyce Ann, my sister, was now 15 or 16. She would go to the nearby grocery store and make eyes at Chuck, the boy about her age behind the meat counter cutting up chickens. His mother, Mrs. Hudson, was the head cashier and couldn't help but notice the two were eyeballing each other. She liked Joyce's looks and would have Chuck deliver our groceries. One thing led to another, and in September of 2009 they will celebrate their 50th wedding anniversary. They have three children.

My son Richard and I lived with Joyce and Chuck for a while in the early years of my marriage to David. They made a room in the basement for us. Richard was a feisty baby. When he would finish a bottle, he would throw it at me. That's when I switched from glass to plastic. It was a lot less bruising. But he was an adorable baby. I'll share more about Richard later.

Joyce's older daughter, Cheri, now serves as a missionary in Africa and is married to a man who is teaching ministers in Africa. Joyce's son David is married and has a child. Joyce's daughter Julie is married and has three daughters.

My brother Alfred finished college and got married and has a son and three daughters.

Then my brother Ward decided after he came home from the Air Force that he would join the Peace Corp, which sent him to Africa. Shortly after his return, I invited him to a party and introduced him to Sandy.

They married and have three daughters; she already had two children from a previous marriage. He helped her raise them as well.

Chapter 13
Miscarriages

A good friend of mine recently had a miscarriage, which reminded me of the three I had in California when I was married to David.

The first miscarriage occurred in 1965. David and I hadn't been married very long. It was in my first trimester. I was disappointed, but because we had so many bills, I don't know how we could have afforded a baby.

A year later, also in the first trimester, I miscarried again. When it was over, I began to worry that I might never be able to carry a baby full term. David was in the service and because I was working two jobs, our finances were in better shape.

The third miscarriage came in 1969. We were trying to hold off having a baby until my body could get stronger. But David was going off to Viet Nam, and I would be alone. Stress . . . stress . . . and more stress.

Now, after *three* miscarriages, I felt for certain I would never carry a baby full term.

What I didn't know then was that when I would get pregnant, *gestational* diabetes would set in. That was why I couldn't carry to full term. And this was the reason for all of my complications later in the births of my sons.

Chapter 14

The Storm Builds

In the beginning of our marriage, Bob didn't mind my making a lot of the decisions and taking over a number of things he had been doing, such as errands, banking, and running the cars in for servicing.

I worked full time and took care of his boys on weekends. Also, we started spending weekends in Wisconsin with his parents.

We had put God on the shelf. We tried a small church for a while, but we weren't being fed spiritually. So we left.

But although we were neglecting God, he gave us a miracle. My son Jacob had two operations on an eye. God healed the eye just before he was to go in for a third operation.

My sister had shown me in *Mt 10:30*, "But the very hairs of your head are all numbered." This was the same God that could heal the sick and make the lame to walk. Yes, God could heal the tumor in Jacob's eye; and he did.

Mk 11:22-23 was a big help at this time. Jesus said to the disciples, "If you only have faith in God, this is the absolute truth -- you can say to this Mount of Olives, 'Rise up and fall into the Mediterranean,' and your command will be obeyed. All that is required is that you really believe and have no doubt."

Back when we were modernizing the *house from hell,* which we did on weekdays, Bob and I would go to Wisconsin on weekends to look after his parents and, in addition, make improvements on their house. They were getting up in years and could no longer make the repairs.

Then Bob's mother suffered a stroke and a heart attack and was confined to a nursing home. This broke my heart. She had been such an active lady who loved her garden and enjoyed cooking. She seemed to live for her grandchildren.

Now it was maintain our house and their house and cook for Bob's father. He was lost without his wife.

We would pick up Bob's boys in McHenry and then go to Twin Lakes, Wisconsin, to pick up Bob's father. Then it was off to Kenosha to visit Bob's mother.

Several Bible quotations came to mind: *Ex 33:14*, "My presence will go with thee." And *Mt 28:20*, "I am with you always."

Mr. Neumann was in and out of the hospital six times in two months. Much of this was during the Big Snow of January 1979. He was my best friend.

The day before he died, I had asked him to come live with us, and he agreed. While I was preparing his room, the hospital called and said, "Come quick. He has taken a turn for the worse." They could not detect a heartbeat or pulse, but he was still talking.

I asked the nurse to go in and say in his ear, "Bob and Judy love you, and they are on their way to be with you."

We had a two-hour drive. I had asked the Lord to please allow us five minutes to tell him we love him. That's exactly how much time we had with him before he died. Yes, he was still talking.

I had spoken with him the day before, asking if he knew the Lord as his personal savior. He told me, "Yes. Who do you think got me through these past few trying years?"

The morning of his funeral, I asked the Lord for a sign. I was awakened at 5:30 in the morning singing "The Lord's Prayer."

"Our Father which art in heaven." Bob thought I was crazy when I said, "That's it." The Lord had given me the sign. *Mk 2:1*, "It was heard that he was in the house."

In July Bob's aunt died.

In August my boys had gone to Cuba for the month to be with their dad. While they were gone, our dog was hit by a car and killed.

In November, my father had died.

Things had gone from bad to worse. We had two houses. We tried to sell the Wisconsin house but the market had dropped; no one could get financing. We had one income but two sets of bills plus child support.

God was trying to get our attention.

I could not handle all the paperwork involved with Mr. Neumann's death, with his house, his parents' medical appointments, and papers for Mrs. Neumann.

No wonder I had had a breakdown and had gone into the hospital to find out why I had not had a period in nine months. I had locked my body up so tight with stress; my body was in a prison.

1 Cor 13:2, "Though I have all knowledge but have not love, I am nothing."

I was so angry with Bob for not helping me share my terrible load. But then why should he? He knew that *Superwoman* lived here.

Spring came, and so did the rains. Our roof shingles blew off; the tree roots grew into the sewer; the sewer backed up into the house. As a last-ditch effort to save our brand new carpet, I had rolled it up. In the process, the lamps got moved off the nightstands and laid on the bed.

They tipped over and burned the shades, the new bedspread, and the sheets -- all the way to the mattress. We put out the fire but couldn't sleep in our bed for days while the water dried.

Carpenter ants ate the back porch, and it fell off the house. The pool wall rotted, and the pump fell in. Bob was over-burdened with repairs, and I was just over-burdened feeling very unloved.

My grandmother was failing. Our relationship had changed dramatically since my teen years. I tried to please her and to make her as comfortable as possible. She needed me, and this was love to me. Bob didn't need me (at least, not in my mind) so therefore he didn't love me. *So I left Bob.*

Dt 6:12, "Then beware, lest you forget the Lord which brought thee forth out of the land of Egypt, from the house of bondage."

Chapter 15

Another Look Back

*L*eaving Bob because "he didn't love me," set me to thinking. Isn't that why I had left David?

David and I had been married only a short while when Don, a buddy of his from southern Illinois, stopped by. Don was home on leave from the "Seabees" branch of the Navy. The "Seabees" became famous during World War II for building Navy installations on islands that had been conquered from the Japanese.

Don quickly regaled David with how great the Navy was, and especially the "Seabees". When he told David that if he joined up, the Navy would send him back to school and then send him to exotic places -- and all the while, he would get paid for it.

David at the time was working in Chicago at the Sears store on Milwaukee Avenue, Irving Park, and Cicero (Six Points). He liked his job, but Don's sales pitch for the Navy and the "Seabees" cast a spell on David, like one who had been hypnotized.

With no consideration for me or for our marriage, David enlisted. Don failed to tell David that when you first join the Navy, there is no housing or allowance for your wife.

Almost before we knew it, David was off to boot camp at the Great Lakes Naval Training Center north of Chicago. And I quickly got busy selling furniture to get us out of debt.

After boot camp we moved to southern California into an 8' x 30' mobile home. I worked two jobs for the first six months.

The first job was for a company with a military contract. After extensive government scrutiny, I was given a top-secret clearance to work on manuals for Navy missiles.

My second job was as a waitress on weekends from 5:30 in the morning until the middle of the afternoon.

It wasn't long, with David's Navy pay and my income from the two jobs that we moved into a furnished apartment with a pool.

Six months later he was sent to Viet Nam. I returned to Chicago to work at the clothing store again, this time as assistant manager.

Mysteriously, throughout David's frequent far-away Navy assignments, we grew to love one another, even though our marriage wasn't based on love.

Our son Richard was born four years after we were married. Because of my three miscarriages, I was very concerned with Richard's birth. He was born two months premature and, with serious lung problems, spent his first month in an incubator.

David and I were living at Port Hueneme, California, a Seabee base about 60 miles north of Los Angeles. I was in my early pregnancy with Richard, and David would come home for lunch and get off work at 4:30.

By my fourth month of pregnancy, one day our next-door neighbors knocked on our door at 11:30 at night. It was the husband, also in the military, holding their three-day-old baby. He said he had to take his wife to the hospital and would I please watch their baby. I said, "Yes", although I couldn't imagine leaving *my* newborn with a stranger.

The husband was a bit pushy and had a lot of nerve. When I told him what I needed for his baby, he said to just buy it and he'd repay me. I said, No, you buy it. I didn't have any transportation, and we didn't have any extra money.

He bought the formula and diapers and told me his wife had had her gall bladder out and was due to be in the hospital for 10 days to recover. I told him to leave the baby with me. No way could he work, take care of the baby, and visit his wife.

When his wife came home from the hospital, she couldn't sit up or get out of bed without help. So now I had a mother and child to take care of. It was another two weeks before she could even hold her baby.

I would stay at their apartment during the day, making breakfast, lunch, and dinner for the mother and caring for the baby, changing it, and feeding it. Thank God the baby was a good sleeper. After fixing their supper, I would go home and fix ours.

The couple had turned my name into the Red Cross as their caregiver, and lo and behold, one day I received a check in the mail from the Red Cross for $140. It was enough for me to buy a crib for Richard. Little did I know that in another three months he would be born.

David's birthday came in August, and he was already back in Viet Nam. No, he wouldn't be here for the birth of our child.

I wrote the following poem; "Far, Far Away You Will Go", in August of 1967, for David's birthday. He was with the "Seabees" in Viet Nam. I was six-months pregnant with Richard. I had no money for a birthday present. I prayed and asked the Lord what I could give him for a gift. This is the result:

Far, Far Away You Will Go

Far, far away you will go
To not even where the "Seabees" know.
Leave your friends and meet the Foe
To a land of heat and never snow,
A land of violence not fit for a soul.
For some fine day you will return,
I see it now I see it clear.
Long awaited for, you will appear.
For all the time we've been apart,
I've held you close within my heart.
Our son you'll see for the first time,
So healthy, masculine and fine.
A man like you he'll make in time.
Go forth and serve our country dear.
I say these words and without fear
I know your love for it is here,
For God is with you where you may go
In the land of War against the Foe.

With David in Viet Nam, I decided to go home to Chicago to live with my mother. In November I had taken a train out to the Largo house in Darien. I did this often, as I always had fun there. I would stay for the weekend and catch a train with Diane and LaDonna on Monday morning, as they both worked in Chicago.

This particular Sunday wasn't like most. I got up and ran to the bathroom, thinking I had had an accident. Little did I know, but my water had broken. I started having contractions. My mother-in-law offered to drive me home. I said, "Yes", and that "I just didn't feel right". We got lost in an industrial park off North Avenue.

I had already alerted my mom and my brother Ward. He was living at the house with Mom and me.

I called West Suburban Hospital in Oak Park, Illinois, for my doctor. They said he was out of town and turned me over to his partner. We had never met, but he sounded sweet on the phone. I asked if I could come in to be checked, that I just didn't feel right. I asked him to keep me overnight so, as a military dependent, I wouldn't have to pay the required $50 for an emergency. He said don't worry, to come right over, and he would check me over for free. It would have cost $25 if I had stayed all night.

By this time my Mom and brother Ward got to the hospital, and I was having regular contractions. The doctor took one look at me and said, "Young lady, you're going to have your baby pretty quick here."

Mom sent Ward home to turn off the roast she had left in the oven. Fifteen minutes later, Richard Anthony Largo was born. To make things worse, he was born *breech*. It was November of 1967.

He had dark hair and a pear-shaped head and was having trouble breathing. They called him a blue baby. He would breathe so fast that it would exhaust him, and he would turn blue. He was taken to a special nursery.

The next day I contracted pneumonia. The other young mothers in the ward seemed to snub me. I think they thought I was an unwed mother.

They sent me home after 10 days, but Richard had to remain in the hospital for 30 days. They kept him in an oxygen enclosure for almost 30 days.

When I would go to see him, because of my poor eyesight, all I could make out was a dark ball of hair. After I brought him home, I examined every finger, toe, and eyelash.

He weighed 6 pounds 2 ounces at birth but had dropped to 5 pounds 8 ounces. I would put his little bottom in my hand, and his head would rest in the crease of my arm, with skinny little legs dangling down -- bird legs.

My mother-in-law said he would get pretty later. This was the wrong thing to say to a new mother. Why, he was already beautiful to me.

I called the Red Cross to notify David of Richard's birth. He called me on Christmas Eve to wish me a safe delivery. They never notified him that his son had been. The year was 1967. I had been due to deliver on January 3.

In addition to Richard's birth, another good thing happened in November of 1967. I didn't give birth in my brother Ward's brand new 1967 Chevy Impala!

Richard's lungs gave us problems until he was eight. We had a dog and had to give it away to a farmer because Richard was allergic to its longhair dander.

At this time I was blessed to have a great Christian baby-sitter named Ruth Kelly. She was a black lady who baby-sat for seven kids, in addition to having seven children of her own. She would play games with the kids and make them a great lunch, all this for only $17.50 a week.

The first time I went to pick up Rich, he said, "Mom, Mom, I want you to meet my friend Darian. Look Mom, he has curly hair like me." Ruth and I locked eyes and smiled. Color wasn't an issue with either Ruth or me. Rich and Darian were like brothers for several years.

During this trying time in my life, and also in Richard's life, David was in Viet Nam. I was living with my mother and brother. My total monthly Navy allowance was only $98.20 a month.

Chapter 16
More Military Memories

Had David really loved me? What about my trip to Hawaii in 1968 to meet David when he returned from Viet Nam for some R&R (rest and recreation)? I was only 22 years old and traveling with Richard, barely three months old.

Traveling with an infant was no easy task. I looked like a packhorse. I had made arrangements for a bassinet on the plane. It was a four-hour flight to Los Angeles and five hours to Hawaii. Baby seat, diaper bag, purse, and luggage. I had even brought a gallon of water, not knowing if a store would be close at hand when I arrived.

Richard and I checked in at the Holiday Inn close to the Honolulu military airport. You could see the planes land from the hotel window. The airport had two landing strips. The "terminal" was only the size of a four-car garage, with a front desk for checking in.

The military kept secret the individual flights from Viet Nam, which arrived every four hours. Since I didn't know when David would arrive, I would pack up the baby and head over to the airport and meet every plane. I did this for two days. I was starting to lose hope.

This would be the first time David would see his son. Little preemie Richard was now weighing in at 17 pounds. I was weighing in at 100 pounds.

Waiting for yet another flight to arrive, wondering if David would be on board, I thought of the potential grief of being a military wife. Just a few days before we started on the Hawaii trip, I had been standing in front of the living room window burping the baby when a car pulled up in front. Some sharply dressed military figures got out of the car. I panicked. Were they coming to tell me David had been killed in Viet Nam?

I put the baby in the bassinet and ran down stairs in my socks. When I got to the bottom step I went up on my tiptoes to see out the little window above the door. I released the dead bolt and swung open the door.

Where are they? The porch was empty. I was still shaking. Then I saw the military figures. They had gone next door. One of them was kissing the girl who lived there. What a relief! I went back upstairs and broke down and cried. I prayed I would never be on the receiving end of tragic news about the fate of my husband.

I met plane after plane for two days. Finally, David's plane arrived. It was a beautiful sunny day. We stopped at one of the lei stands that line the airport entrance. We bought a "Lei" for each of us.

We stayed one night at the Holiday Inn. The next day we rented a Volkswagen. It was a stick shift, and David had never driven a stick shift. We couldn't figure out how to get it in reverse. When a VW pulled in next to us at a hamburger stand, we asked the driver how to get it in reverse. He showed us. Relief!

Superwoman doesn't live here anymore

We moved into a furnished apartment that looked like it had been built in the 1940s. The furnishings also appeared to be from the 1940s. The landlady was sweet, saying she got a lot of Navy families. She told me of an older woman baby-sitter who lived nearby who was very responsible. We quickly engaged her services for the evening.

We decided to go to the international market place just around the block from where we were staying. We wanted a romantic dinner, and the Don Ho Show was playing at the restaurant. "Tiny Bubbles" was his big hit.

David was trying very hard to be a good dad and be involved. The first time he fed the baby -- carrots -- it required a bath and soaking and washing the outfit he was wearing.

The end of the R&R came too soon, and I watched his plane take off, not knowing if he would ever come home. It wasn't easy to watch the news daily and see all that was being reported. David's job was building landing strips. He had worked at Da Nang, Phu Bai, and at various other places, all of which were on the news frequently.

Richard and I were to leave on a flight to San Francisco at 8:30 at night. The packhorse (me) showed up at the gate with baby, baby chair, diaper bag, purse, and one large suitcase. The ticket agent looked at my San Francisco ticket and took pity on me. He helped me onto the plane, putting us into one of the unoccupied first-class seats.

A lady approached and said, "You're in my seat."

I said, "No I'm not, the agent put me here."

She went for the hostess (now called flight attendants), who looked at my ticket and agreed -- I was in the right seat.

But now the irate lady brought the pilot, who looked at my ticket. He said to me, "You're in the right seat but you're on the *wrong flight*. Your flight just took off."

What had happened was, that kind and considerate ticket agent had put me on a plane to Los Angeles instead of on my flight to San Francisco. But as it turned out, this was a plus. At San Francisco, I would have had a four-hour layover to catch a flight to Chicago. In Los Angeles, I would have only a two-hour wait.

I told the pilot, "The ticket agent put me on this plane and in this seat, and I'm not leaving."

The pilot discreetly settled the problem by putting the angry lady in a different first-class seat.

But I was soon wishing I had been placed on the correct flight -- to San Francisco. As it turned out, the entire Don Ho cast was on board. They had just finished putting on a show in Honolulu and were en route to Los Angeles to put on another show.

They partied all night long. I was running on very little sleep and a good case of nerves. They were so loud; I thought they would wake my baby. The hostess already doesn't like me because I had been a problem from the start of her day.

With David spending so much time in Viet Nam, it was like not even being married. Had he loved me? I thought of my spending some time with David on, of all places, Midway Island.

David was assigned to Midway with no housing available for us. Another family gave us their house so Richard and I could come there. We stayed for about two months.

By this time Richard was 18 months old. I hadn't seen David since the Hawaii visit, over a year earlier.

This time on the long flights, Richard was like a can of worms. Just try keeping a toddler in a seat for the four-hour flight to Los Angeles, the five-hour flight to Hawaii, and the five-hour flight to Midway, the last flight being on a military supply plane.

At Midway, David and I luckily got to stay in the furnished house of a family that was going away on leave.

Midway Island is a strange place. It's only seven miles long and four miles wide. It has beautiful beaches but not a lot of grass. A man-made coral reef extends all around the island. The beaches have crystal-clear water. Guard towers allow warnings for when sharks are sighted.

The best part of staying at Midway was when the ship came in once a month bringing food, milk, and all kinds of knickknacks from China.

But the oddest things about the place are the gooney birds and the roaches.

The black-and-white gooney birds, part of the albatross family, are beautiful in flight, but are terribly inefficient in landing. They tend to trip upon landing, often breaking their necks. Hundreds of them die daily. They have an intricate mating dance where they clack their beaks up at the sky, drop them down under their wings, and make a loud honk.

And the island was swarming with roaches. They were about an inch long -- big enough to make you uncomfortable just thinking about them. One of the military men was the designated exterminator, and he would show up daily. We would wipe all the counters and sinks down at night and again in the morning with bleach.

There was a door one inch off the floor on a closet under the stairs, and I was told that a lizard was alive in there killing any roach that made it past the front door.

The house was nicely furnished with bamboo or rattan furniture. Each closet had a light bulb on 24 hours a day to discourage the roaches.

Midway gets frequent storms with high winds. The palm trees would bend until you thought they would break. The next morning they would right themselves. I found out why they could do this. They have a very shallow root system that goes down in the sand and attaches itself to a rock.

As the years went by, remembering those palm trees would help me get through times of trial. To weather my own personal storms, I would always try to remember to attach my roots onto the rock of my salvation, the Lord Jesus Christ.

When Richard and I arrived home in Illinois, to prevent the possibility of bringing roaches into the house, I unpacked on the driveway. Everything had to be washed before bringing it inside.

Chapter 17
Jacob Is Born

Two years later David was back at Great Lakes to attend a service school. Richard and I moved in with him on the base. Then he was assigned to another school in Falls Church, Virginia, near Washington, DC.

Before vacating our Great Lakes apartment, it was given a white-gloves inspection. The more things that were found wrong, the more you paid.

Richard and I joined David at Falls Church as soon as he was able to acquire housing. It was a brand new apartment, but unfurnished. We managed somehow to acquire enough used furniture to get by. I was about eight-months pregnant.

Richard, now four years old, soon acquired a little friend named Gina, who lived with her family right across the hall. Her family was not military; her father was an air traffic controller at Dulles International Airport, Dulles, Virginia. His wife was a stay-at-home mom. She was very creative in the way she kept up their apartment.

One day while Richard and Gina were outside playing, Gina's mother pounded on my front door. I opened it and there she stood crying. Gina was screaming. Richard was choking on a hard piece of candy. He was turning blue.

I knew the fire department would never make it in time. First I tried to reach the obstacle with my fingers, but the object would only spin.

Next I tried hitting him on the back, hoping to pop it out. It didn't. Then I grabbed him by the ankles and shook him, to no avail.

Suddenly I remembered that our hot-water bottle, still in the box, had a hose attachment. I ran to the linen closet, tore open the box and pushed the hose down Richard's throat and blew. It worked and saved his life. His breathing returned to normal.

Now I'm striving to calm Gina's mom. She was just a mess.

I put Richard in the car and drove him to Bethesda Naval Hospital, 20 minutes away. The doctor examined him and said he was fine. I told him what I had done.

"Whatever made you think of that?"

"Well, I knew that when a baby is born, they run a tube down its throat to clear out the fluids. I figured if I did any damage with the tube, at least he would live. As it was, without air, he would have died."

During my next weekly appointment with my doctor -- this time at Bethesda Naval Hospital, he listened to my belly. I had gained 46 pounds, and diabetes had set in. I had been advised to slow down, but that was a hard thing to do with a four-year-old in the house. The doctor ordered me down the hall for an X-ray. He suspected I was carrying twins.

The hospital was huge. It had tape on the floor to each department. Blue tape meant follow it and you'd be in X-ray. Red was for blood work. I had been there often enough. I don't know what yellow or green meant.

The hall was long; it had brick that came up about four feet on both sides, and eight-foot windows running up to the ceiling. The sun was shining, and it was August, and a very hot summer. Thank God for the air-conditioning. I was so nervous as I put on a gown for the X-ray. I was talking out loud to myself. Then I had a talk with God.

"Surely you wouldn't give me *two* more babies. How would I manage? I only have enough things for one. Two babies and a four-year-old -- I'll go nuts. Besides, David is going back to Viet Nam. How can I afford to feed them?" But then I thought, Oh, but it would be so nice to dress them alike.

Finally I said, "Lord, it's in your hands. Just remember, you said you wouldn't give me more than I could handle."

I don't know why the Lord would even listen to my prayer. I hadn't given him any time in over a year.

They handed me the X-ray to give to the doctor. I couldn't resist. I undid the string on the big brown envelope and took out the X-ray. I stopped in the long hallway with the big windows to take a look. I thought I was alone. I just had to know.

A doctor came up behind me and said, "Looks like twins to me."

I was so embarrassed for getting caught sneaking a look at the X-ray before the doctor had seen it. But what woman in her right mind wouldn't have peeked? The doctor said, "If you don't deliver by Sunday, come in early and we'll get you started."

David didn't really react to the news. He was more interested in a football game in Washington that Saturday. David had talked to one of the aides next door, that if I went into labor, would he drive me to the hospital? His lack of caring just showed me that he didn't really care about family or me.

On Sunday morning at about 9 o'clock, David drove me to the hospital. Richard stayed with Mary, a neighbor who was married to a marine. She was from Taiwan and had an 18-month-old daughter. She assured me not to worry, that she would watch him very carefully. She added that Richard was very gentle with her little girl.

The hospital had had a power failure, and an emergency generator was supplying electricity only for essential uses. Although it was a hot summer day, air-conditioning was not considered essential.

They wheeled me to a small delivery room at about 3 o'clock in the afternoon. The doctor was at my feet, the nurse on my right, and I don't know who the lady was on my left. The doctor had the nurse strap a can of Sodium Pentothal on my arm.

The first baby weighed 6 pounds 2 ounces, but was stillborn. When the doctor told me, I said, "That's okay. God knows what I can handle."

Then Jacob arrived at just under 10 pounds, stripping and severely damaging the veins in the birth canal. I lost a lot of blood, and the doctor nearly lost me on the birthing table. He spent the next 2½ hours stitching up those veins to stop the hemorrhaging. They kept bringing in bags of blood.

"Who will deliver me from this body of death?" *Romans 7:24*

With my eyes closed, I experienced God's presence. I was looking down from the ceiling. There was a tunnel with a white light at the far end. I saw a brilliant white glow. A soft voice was calling my name. *Judy . . . Judy . . . Judy.* It sounded almost like my grandmother. But Gram was still alive.

"In him was life, and the life was the light of men." *John 1:4*

The spirit of death was in that room. The air-conditioning had gone out, and it was 95 degrees. The expectant mother before me had died, but her twins had lived.

God had revealed his place to me. I was different. God was real.

I could hear what was being said in the delivery room. They were doing all they could to save me. A doctor entered the room and said, "Is she going to make it?"

I zoomed right back into my body and said, "I sure as hell hope so."

"Oh, sorry. I didn't know you were awake," the other doctor said.

I opened my eyes. My doctor was staring daggers at him.

With the complications, it would be a while before I could go home. David brought Rich to see me, but he wasn't allowed in my room. So David put him in a waiting room and came with a wheelchair to get me.

Rich said, "What did they do, Mom? Break your legs?"

"No, Honey. I'm just weak. Don't worry. I'll get better."

When I got home, I was so weak. I had to sit to make dinner. My two sisters-in-law came for a visit. They wanted to wake the baby just to see him. I was depressed by now and not doing very well.

David wasn't much help. He had had two tours of duty in Viet Nam and would be leaving the following June to go back for another two years.

Our marriage was in trouble. In fact, it had floundered from the day David enlisted in the Navy without telling me. I thought I was in a marriage forever, but now I could see that this just wouldn't happen.

God had been missing in our lives since we got married. I had gone to church when David was gone, but he wouldn't go when he returned.

Our marriage had gone from hopeful to hopeless. Alcohol and abuse had moved in, and I had moved out. Once again I cried out to the Lord for help, and his peace came over me like a dome.

"I will cry to you when my heart is overwhelmed. Lead me to the rock that is higher than I." *Ps. 61:2*

I was very close to God when I was going to leave David. It was a Sunday evening in our apartment in Falls Church, Virginia, six months after Jacob was born. David had been out all afternoon drinking at a bar. He didn't get home until almost 7 o'clock. He asked me to fix him a roast beef sandwich.

Rich, 4 years old, was still up. I remember talking to David and asking what he wanted on the sandwich. I had a long butcher knife in my hand. It was flashing in my eyes.

David yelled at Rich and kicked the coffee table at the same time. Had I not reacted quickly, it would have hit Rich in the back of the neck. I pulled Rich up with my left hand. I told him to go on to bed, that I would be in to tuck him in, in a minute.

I turned to David. I was very angry. Then I turned abruptly and went into the kitchen. I slammed the knife on the counter. I opened the dishwasher and said, "God help me."

I slid the knife into the dishwasher and locked it down. I stood there and said, "God, keep me from killing him. You gave me two beautiful boys. Don't let me go to jail."

I went back into the living room. It was as though a dome were over me. I spoke in a calm voice.

"In two weeks I am taking the boys and the gold Dodge Challenger and going back to Chicago. I want a divorce, and I don't care if you send money or not, because God will supply. The things in this house are yours. I'll just take Jacob's crib. I don't want anything else. The rest of the things you can sell or give away."

I called my sister and asked her to look for a one-bedroom apartment. She found one, and two weeks later I drove home with the boys.

David had asked me not to get a divorce until he came back from Viet Name after two years. Not because he didn't want a divorce, but the military would pay an allotment and medical for the boys. I had two boys to raise. I needed a job and a place to live. But I wasn't worried. I knew that dome would stay with me and protect me and supply the needs for the boys and me.

David and I separated, and the boys and I moved back to Illinois from Washington. I found an apartment in Hanover Park and had the first-month's rent and security deposit for a year's lease, not knowing where or how I would pay the second month.

My furniture was a crib, high chair, rollaway bed from my mom, two chairs from my sister, and a $15 oak antique kitchen set. These were gifts from God.

I found a job working two days a week in the apartment complex office. In addition, I baby-sat for seven children while their mothers partied. They would supply a one-pot meal to feed all the kids and myself, and

I would bed them down in sleeping bags on the floor for the night. The mothers would bring a box of cereal and a gallon of milk to feed the children, who would get picked up by 10 o'clock.

I was invited to join the ladies as they partied, but I refused. They called me "the little nun."

"For sin shall not have dominion over you, for you are not under law but under grace." *Romans 6:14*

David didn't have time for me. Later on, Bob didn't have time for me either. Why not? Was there something wrong with me?

Or was it a shortcoming in each of them that robbed them of the ability to love?

Jacob had learned to swim in Washington at Water Babies and was now *18 months*. I couldn't believe it but it was true -- he was actually *going off the high-dive*.

A mishap when I was six years old had ingrained a fear of water into me. My sister, Joyce, and I had gone to the Forest Park swimming pool with my friend Diane Lightfoot, her brothers, cousin, and Ramona, another friend. I was walking next to the water at the deep end when two teenagers pushed me in. I couldn't swim. Fortunately, Diane's dad saw what happened and jumped in and saved me. This put a fear of water in me until I was 21 living in California.

A lady living in the apartment complex trying out for the Olympic team; taught me how to swim and dive. This is the reason I had taught my sons to swim at a very early age. I didn't want them to grow up with a fear of water as I had.

I would often spend time in the evening reflecting on David. He had alcoholism in his background. Had I known that David was to fall victim, I likely would not have married him. But at age 18, what kind of wisdom does a girl have?

Chapter 18

A Fresh Start

I said God would provide, and he did. He opened doors left and right.

The boys and I got settled quickly in our new apartment back in Hanover Park, Illinois. It was in a complex with a lot of other apartments. There seemed to be quite a few other single mothers.

Right away I started baby-sitting and soon was sitting with as many as seven children at a time. The girls would bring supper and breakfast, and I would have the little ones camp out on my living-room rug.

Soon the manager of the apartment complex asked if I would fill in for him two days a week. When I learned that many of the apartment occupants were party animals, I started making and selling trays of hors d'oeuvres. They soon became in big demand.

But after nine months in the complex, it seemed to be deteriorating as a healthy place for my boys. We moved to an apartment in Waukegan, located north of Chicago and right next to Great Lakes. I was still a military wife and allowed medical treatment at military facilities.

I applied for a job as manager of a boutique. I already had a sitter -- Ruth Kelly, whom I had used for Richard earlier.

Then my divorce came through. As I walked out of court, I heard a radio off in the distance and the song, *"I Can See Clearly Now."*

I was now legally free of David. Would I really see clearly now? Had I learned my lesson?

It hadn't been all bad, there was Hawaii, Midway Island, and, best of all, Richard and Jacob, my precious little boys.

I loved our new apartment. It was in a secure building with a pool, which would mean entertainment for the boys and me.

We had a lot of quality time walking along the Lake Michigan beach, picnicking, collecting rocks to paint, and shells to create little animals.

They were the best little boys ever. They were very happy, with lots of laughs. But best of all, we were now going to church and Sunday School weekly.

God was not only keeping us safe, but he was also supplying our every need.

Soon a young lady, a struggling Christian, came to me and asked if she could move in. She did, and the grocery bill eased up. But what I didn't know was that she was dating a Navy man who was involved in a satanic cult. But God protected us.

On Richard's sixth birthday, I got him a cross on a chain for him to wear around his neck. This was something that would be his and his alone, something he wouldn't have to share with baby-sitters or with the children with whom I sat.

One night I had a date and left the boys with the young lady roommate. When I returned and checked on Richard, his chain and cross were gone. They were never found.

My roommate broke up with the boyfriend and moved to Florida, where she had a nervous breakdown. It wasn't until later that year I learned her sailor boyfriend had been involved with the occult.

"And have no fellowship with the unfruitful works of darkness, but rather expose them." *Eph. 5:11*

My dating didn't look promising. But why should it? After all, I hadn't asked for God's help. No wonder I was finding only un-Godly men.

Now that I was divorced, I was no longer eligible to receive medical care at Great Lakes. A friend who knew of my financial struggle told me of a job opening as manager of the Wheatherfield Gardens Apartments complex in Schaumburg. There were 136 units in 10 buildings. In addition to the salary, it had yet another perk: a free apartment. I applied and got the job.

I saw this as the golden opportunity to meet and land *Mr. Right*. Thirty to forty people a day would come to the apartment complex looking for an apartment. And Richard would be only three blocks from school. Jacob was spending a lot of time in a nursery right behind the building.

I was wearing a mask to hide the insecure; unworthy person I felt I was. So I put on a face and attitude that was happy, secure, positive, very sure of myself. My bosses bought it and were impressed with my performance and rewarded me with good pay.

I negotiated a contract and convinced them they would make more money if they rented out my apartment and I lived in the model apartment. This would mean free rent, free utilities, a salary, and in three years the model furniture would become mine. They could write the furniture off on taxes, and they bought it. The boys and I were on Easy Street. *Superwoman* lived here!

Somehow, life didn't seem complete, although we were attending weekly church and Sunday school. In addition, our neighborhood Bible study met in my apartment weekly so I wouldn't have to pay a baby-sitter unnecessarily.

"Meditate within your heart on your bed, and be still." *Ps. 4:4*

After one of our meetings, I sat down on my bed and cried out to the Lord. "Please, Lord, give me a husband, someone to love me and to love my children, someone to come home to us at night."

When you ask the Lord for something, be sure it's what you really want, because he really does answer prayer.

Chapter 19
Jim

It was 1980. After divorcing Bob, the boys and I moved out of the house in Hanover Park and moved to a condo. Rich was now 14, and Jacob was 10. I was not a happy camper. In fact, I was feeling very needy.

Bob had buried himself in work, which was his way of coping with his second divorce.

One day I got to talking with a neighbor in another condo. His name was Jim. He had a listening ear, and I had a lot to say.

He was nothing like other men I had dated. He was short, bearded, with blondish-brown, silky hair. His gentle, beautiful, baby blue eyes distracted from his weathered face and nicotine-stained teeth. His bulbous nose was sending out a signal that he was a drinker, but I missed it.

Although he was actually rather nice looking, he seemed to be very strong-willed, with a chip on his shoulder. Yet, he seemed somehow, despite his rugged exterior, to be gentle and kind. Also, he seemed to be very wise.

He had a great personality and lots and lots of friends. He was outgoing and loved to fish and hunt. He enjoyed gardening and canning or freezing everything he grew.

Although he appeared to be in good health, he had had cancer, which was in remission, and he was divorced.

He was a carpenter by trade, but had been a contractor. When business went bad, he took a job as a machinist working nights.

He had stayed in touch with his three sons, but had practically lost touch with his daughter, who had sided with his ex-wife.

We had known each other for a year when he asked me to marry him. I said "Yes", and we were supposed to marry in August. We decided to marry at a justice of the peace and have a reception at the Villa Olivia Country Club in Bartlett.

But we had not been getting along well, and I canceled the wedding. Since we had received commitments for several thousand dollars for the reception, we decided to go ahead with it. After all, no one but Jim and I would know we hadn't actually got married.

I had gained considerable weight -- out of frustration. I had shopped for a dress at the last minute and found an old-fashioned long dress with lots of lace in ecru, and in addition a big floppy hat that I doctored up with flowers and lace.

The reception took place the next day, and no one was any the wiser. I must admit, I felt a bit adventurous and reckless, enjoying my own wedding reception but having canceled the wedding.

Now it was October. We decided once again to get married. On October 8, it was a cool fall day with the leaves beginning to turn colors with signs of fall all around.

On the way to the JP in downtown Wheaton, I had a gut feeling. A little voice in the back of my head kept saying, *"Don't do it. Don't do it."*

I kept thinking, if I back out at the last minute, it would really embarrass him. He seemed somewhat excited. As the judge asked us to repeat the vows, I once again didn't heed the little voice in my head. Instead of saying, *"I don't,"* I said, *"I do."*

The moment I said it, I knew I made a big mistake. But I pushed aside my regrets and decided I would somehow make the best of it.

We left the courthouse and took a ride to the Morton Arboretum in Lisle. We drove through the trees, plants, and waterways. We stopped and walked hand in hand through the woods. I kept thinking what I had just done. Gotten married! I pushed back an ominous feeling of dread.

Next we went to a Pancake House for brunch. Then, back to the condo. We had decided that I would give up my condo and move into Jim's condo. It had two bedrooms; the boys would share one, and Jim and I, the other.

Superwoman doesn't live here anymore

Jim and my son Rich did not get along. Rich, being a teenager, thought he knew it all. Jacob, on the other hand, was 9, and impressionable and easy-going and could get along with anyone. Rich felt out of place and missed his friends back around the house where we had lived in Hanover Park.

Rich had asked if he could live with Bob and my brother Ward, who were now living in that house. I said no, we were living here now.

Jim had done his own decorating. The condo was ultramodern with quality furniture. It was very clean, and everything had its place -- all the time. He loved homemade meals and didn't care much for eating out.

Within days of our wedding, Jim told me I no longer needed to work. He had money, and wanted me to stay home. That sounded good at first. But it closed me in.

At first he was loving and kind. But he had a drinking habit I wasn't aware of. When he'd start drinking, a whole other side of him showed up. He became demanding, selfish, and mean. It took me three months to see this other side.

I was told; I didn't need my friends calling the house. I had him. I was also told; I didn't need my family anymore. I had him. Jim and I were now *family*. That was all I needed.

I became a possession, not a wife. While he was working nights, he'd pin my car in so I couldn't go anywhere. I was beginning to feel like I was in jail. I had just signed on for a life sentence. I could feel jail cell bars all around me.

When he drank, it got worse. One night after he had been drinking, we got into an argument. With a gun in his hand, he chased me around the kitchen table and said, "If you're still here in the morning when I get home from work, you'll be dead." I believed him. This was no time to test the waters.

My sister-in-law Sandy was in Chicago visiting her parents. Scared to death, I called her. She helped me move my furniture out that night.

He came looking for me. I hid. I changed jobs. I got an apartment and prayed he wouldn't find me.

He didn't, and $10,000 later, I was divorced. He had property and had money, but I knew if I paid for the divorce and didn't ask for a dime, he would sign on the dotted line. He did.

There is a verse in the Bible that talks about sin feeling good for only a season. I knew from the beginning I should have said, *"I don't."* But I didn't. And yet, God protected my children and me.

Talk about a whirlwind marriage and a whirlwind divorce. From start to finish, we were married *five months.* And yet, thinking back about Jim, he wasn't all bad. He was a craftsman and built custom pieces for beautiful homes. Using his skills, he had built a dollhouse for me. This wasn't just any dollhouse. It was a nine-room Victorian dollhouse. Over the years, Bob installed electrical wiring in it, and I furnished and decorated it. After owning it for 28 years, in the summer of 2008, I gave it to my niece Alison. It was time to move on.

His mother, Julia, made me a beautiful afghan as a welcoming gift to the family. I still have it today. Julia and Jim's father had lived in Chicago and got divorced and both remarried. With his second wife, Jim's father ended up living across the street from Julia, who in the meantime married a man named Joe Myka. Julia was a beautiful, petite lady who looked like a million bucks. Her second husband had silver white hair and was tall, towering over Julia.

After our brief marriage Jim, whose real name was Marion, moved in with his mother. His father had been an alcoholic, and that was the reason for their divorce. Julia went on to have two more sons. By the time I met Jim, he too had been married and divorced.

His ex-wife lived in Wisconsin, and that is where his daughter lived. His three sons were also living in Wisconsin when we met. The oldest son, David, was married and had a daughter and son. Eric, the middle son, got married in Wisconsin and moved to Joliet, Illinois. The youngest son, Kyle, had a daughter, and along came twin girls.

The boys all followed in their father's footsteps -- they loved to fish and hunt. Kyle was very talented in wood-turnings and cabinet making. Each son was good-looking and seemed to be very smart.

I had written them a letter in the beginning so they would know what to expect of me. I was simply their father's wife; I wasn't trying to take their mother's place. I couldn't, and they wouldn't have to walk on eggshells in front of me. I was there to love and support their dad.

Judith Neumann-Dicks

My reason for writing the letter was that my father had remarried, and Ruth had left the four of us out of their lives. I wouldn't do that.

Shortly after separating from Jim, I went to work on the night shift at the Patient Research Center in Lombard. One night I wrote the following:

Night Shift

In the stillness of morning I sit and wait,
Waiting for the sun to rise
And the day to break into joy.

The cars pass with lights
And no faces in the blackened windshields.
The lights of night timed to go off,
And for the moment nothing is happening.

Soon the day will begin,
And the phone will ring,
The door will slide open,
And people of the morning
In a hurry, hurry to start
The beginning of the rest of their lives.

The flowers go unadmired,
Birds sing a silent song
To the sound of cars and trucks in motion.
The blue sky still muted
By smoke stacks and semi-trucks.
The sun warms the dew and the grass gets greener.

Stop -- Stop, take a look around you,
All that God has created for you.
Look at what you have created for him.

Life passes by too fast;
Take the time to thank him daily.
Take the time to see the flowers in their beauty,
Take the time to see a sunrise,
Take the time to look up and reach out
And love one another.

For God created you and me.
Over and above all the gifts he gave,
He gave us love.
Even when the birds don't sing,
The flowers don't bloom,
And the sun doesn't rise,
We will still have one another.

So, stop, my love, and let me love you,
For you are God's creation,
And I want to enjoy every moment,
For life is too short,
And I don't want to miss out on a moment.

By loving him, we can not only
Share this life together,
But have everlasting life together.

Chapter 20

Remarrying Bob

Now I had three marriages behind me. Three reasons to feel sorry for myself, *David* hadn't loved me, *Bob* was too busy for me, and now, *Jim* loved to control me, and, of course, Roy the rapist hadn't loved me. My self-image was in bad shape. BAD shape!

I was once again back to square one. But I knew *my boys* loved me. Although my ex-husbands didn't need me, Rich and Jacob did. I couldn't solve my problems the easy way -- kill myself. No. Rich and Jacob needed me, and I hung on to that as my lifeline.

And one more thing kept me afloat. I knew that somehow, through it all, *God* loved me. Yes, he did. But I had been neglecting him. Where had God been when I needed him? Where had I been?

Feeling down on myself got me to thinking about Norma. Now there was a woman who had reason -- I should say *reasons* -- to feel sorry for herself.

I met Norma when I held my first garage sale, which happened to be at the *pink* house. As it turned out, it was the first of my annual garage sales. Holding them each year thereafter became a way to help myself stay organized.

It was a very hot summer day. Joyce, my sister, was helping me. A woman carrying a sickly looking boy approached. The boy looked to be about six years old, but actually he was 11 or 12.

We offered the lady a chair, and she asked for a glass of water. We got one for her and for her son. She introduced herself as Norma. She had a sweet southern accent and said she was from Kentucky. She was looking for items for poor families in Kentucky, but she also bought old furniture and fixed it up -- she said she was good at it --and sold it as a way of making extra income.

She said she had three sons, that the other two were a little older, in their teens. Her father was a minister, and she seemed to be a lovely Christian.

A few years passed, and Bob and I had moved to our big, white house on Laurel. It was time for the annual garage sale, which had grown into an *event.* I started involving my family and friends.

We would have breakfast and lunch in the garage, and they would add their items into the sale. It would bring in several hundred dollars, which became my income, since I was no longer working outside the home. This would help pay for school supplies and new clothes for the startup of the school year.

It was the middle of the afternoon when Norma came, dressed very nicely, with three other ladies. I wondered where her son was.

"Norma, how are you?" I said.

"Not too well. We are coming from my son's funeral. I guess you probably think I'm nuts, and maybe I am, but I just can't go home right now."

I told her I understood, and I hugged her.

"Come and sit down," I said. "What happened?"

I thought she had referred to the little guy she had been carrying when I last saw her.

"No, it wasn't my youngest son. It was my 19-year-old. The little guy died a few years ago."

I thought how could God let this happen? Let this poor woman lose two of her sons?

She said he had been at the quarry in Elgin with his friends and had drowned. She thought it had been foul play, because when they brought up his body, he had a look of terror in his eyes.

A few more years passed, and once again I was having the annual garage sale. Here comes Norma.

"Hi, Norma. How are you doing?" I asked.

She looked worried or depressed. I wasn't sure which -- both, as it turned out.

"I'm worried about my 18-year-old. He's depressed over his two brothers dying. He doesn't think *he* should still be around either. I don't know that I could take losing him too, and I'm afraid for him."

After closing the garage sale, I got to thinking about her son. I know that has to be the worse thing ever -- to bury your children. I talked nonstop to the Lord that night.

The next morning I went to church, and Bob stayed home. As I sat there and prayed, certain verses came into my head. As they did, I would write them down. I no sooner would do this than the pastor would say turn to a verse, and it was the one I just wrote down. This happened *10 times!*

When we got up to sing, I noticed Dave Howard standing behind me. He had been a missionary and worked for the Billy Graham Crusade.

I knew he walked with God, so I asked him to pray with me for Norma's son.

When I got home I asked Bob to go with me to Norma's. He said no, he wasn't feeling good, but that he would pray for him, that I should go alone.

I called Norma and asked if her son was home. She said, "Yes", and I asked if I could come over.

Entering her living room, there was a large bar (one of her garage sale finds). I thought I didn't want to sit there and tower over her son, so I went to the coffee table and knelt down. The lighting was dim, and my eyes weren't so good. The sunlight was shinning on the Bible.

Her son entered, and I greeted him with a handshake. He sat down on the barstool.

I said, "God has sent me here today with a message for you. I don't know what it means, but I have to deliver it to be obedient to him. What you do with it is between you and him. There are 10 verses he wants me to share."

I turned the pages of my Bible and read them in a clear, steady voice, even though I hate reading aloud. When I was done, I said, "I don't know what they mean."

He said, "I do," and he hugged me and said thank-you.

That night he got on his motorcycle and was doing 80 on Lake Street. He lost control, hit a pole, and was hurled through the air. When he came down, he landed without breaking a single bone. The police came and said they had never seen anything like it, that he should have been dead.

He told his mother that the reason he wasn't dead was because of that lady who had stopped by. Norma knew it was the Lord who had saved him, not me.

I had put the young man in God's hands that afternoon, and God wasn't going to let go -- ever.

I needed an income. So I started a business in Barrington called the "Finishing Touch." It was inside a beauty shop. I would do makeup, nails, eyebrow arching, and body wraps, using horse liniment and then wrapping the person in plastic wrap for an hour. I would have them drink lots of water to help them lose inches. It was fun, and my high prices gave me the income I needed for the boys and me.

I started attending the Keeneyville Bible Church every Sunday. John, the pastor, right away discerned that I was carrying a massive burden. Unhappiness reflected from my eyes. He kept telling me, "We need to talk." I would say, yes, but I put off meeting with him for a whole year.

In the meantime, I started seeing Bob again. I think I realized deep inside that, God had handpicked him for me, and that without him life wasn't worth living. We tried counseling with an organization in Oregon, Illinois, called New-Life or New Lebon. It would have worked, but we weren't ready to listen.

I finally made an appointment with John. It was worth it. Boy, was it worth it. I poured out my guts. I swear I used a box of Kleenex.

John then wanted to meet with Bob and me together. So I arranged for an appointment. Did John ever *put our heads on straight!*

Here's what Bob and I learned and what we started to practice from that moment on -- that God revealed in Genesis:

- God is first.
- The husband is head of the house over the wife and children and answerable to God.
- The wife is partner to the husband, over the children, and answerable to the husband and to God.
- The children obey the parents and are answerable to the parents and to God.
- It was so simple!

- We learned that when you marry, you become one: one body, one spirit, and one mind.
- You wouldn't cut off a part of your own body. So don't cut off your husband; he is part of your body.
- Here are a few more things Bob and I learned:
- Work together on all things.
- Communicate.
- Never accuse. This builds walls that will never come down.
- Fight fair. Stick to the problem at hand and never bring up old issues.
- Never go to bed mad. Don't let the sun go down on your wrath.
- Put God first, and all these other things will fall into place.
- Read the Bible. It's the best book ever written.
- "Wives submit . . . Husbands love . . . Children obey . . ." *Eph 5:22, 25, 6:1*
- "Behold, I stand at the door and knock. If anyone hears my voice and opens the door, I will come in to him and sup with him and he with me." *Rev. 3:20*

It was as though I had received the following words from the Lord:

- Put God first and all these other things will fall into place. What I really want for you is hope for tomorrow and the best life ever, every day.
- Put your feet on the right path, and you'll always know where you've been and where you're going.

Bob and I were remarried in a private ceremony. Pastor John performed the rites in our living room. The reception was a home-cooked meal in our family room, with a few family members present. I moved back into the house where I used to live with him -- the house he had never left.

We became *one* when we were married and now we needed to function as one in *agreement.* We began to function with God first, and for God to be considered in ALL decisions.

God had moved in; *Superwoman* had moved out.

Bob was the head of our household. This was his God-given right.

"Stand fast in one spirit, with one mind striving together for the faith of the gospel." Phil 1:27

Yes, I was loved. God loved me, and he was no respecter of persons. Even though I had been held back to repeat the first grade, God didn't care.

I could take off the mask, because God knew what was on the inside. I couldn't hide anything from him. No, I didn't have to be the best, because God loved me *as I am*. The more I realized this, the more Bob could see Christ in me, and the more he responded to that love.

God showed me I didn't have to carry everybody's burden, that he is stronger. Why didn't I just turn things over to him?

Our boys began to see forgiveness and love move into our home and they, in turn, began responding to God.

Superwoman had moved out and made way for God to move in -- without even redecorating.

I reflected back on my leaving Bob to end our first marriage. I hadn't felt loved. He had been neglecting me. *We* had been neglecting God.

Now, in our second marriage, I felt loved. Bob no longer neglected me. We were not neglecting God. We became active in our church.

We became members of the Gideon Society and went around together passing out Bibles. We went to hospitals. The white New Testaments went to the doctors and the nursing staff; the gold ones went to the hospital workers. Blue ones were for sharing with anyone. Orange Bibles went to college students; red ones went to Catholics; and green ones went to the military.

Bob was the keeper of the Bibles until we distributed them. At times we had as many as 50,000 Bibles in our home. Our spare room was literally filled with Bibles.

One day, Jacob's friends dropped by. From 20 to 30 boxes of Bibles were in the front hall; I hadn't moved them to the spare room yet. The friend said, "What's all this?"

Something prompted me to tell him, "I took an Evelyn Wood speed-reading course, and this is a week's worth of books for me to read." He was shocked.

We made friends with a number of members of the Gideon Society, among them, Barbara Hansen and her husband, Arnie. We used to meet them and several other couples regularly at the Old Country Buffet.

In distributing the Bibles, we followed a protocol. The men would leave the Bibles in hotels, motels, and in hospital rooms and doctors' waiting rooms. The women members of Gideons, the Auxiliary, would distribute Bibles in only certain areas of hospitals.

Protocol finds its place in many endeavors, even into the Gideons. One day we were in Central Du Page Hospital when one of the male leaders asked if I would place a Bible in a waiting room down the hall. I did, and his wife, a real stickler for rules and regulations, said, "What did you just do?"

"I placed a Bible in that waiting room."

"Dear, you're not supposed to do that. That's the men's job."

I replied, "It was your husband who asked me to do it."

I should have left it at that, but I kept talking. "When my husband and I got married, we became one, so you could say it was his feet and my hands that placed that Bible. I didn't think the Lord would care who placed it. It would seem to me he would be more concerned with who read it."

To become a member of Gideons, you needed to hold a management position or be an owner of a business. It was the members that supported the cost of the Bibles. In addition, a monthly dinner and meeting were held in each county to raise funds to defer the cost of the Bibles.

Chapter 21

Bob's Cancer

Bob and I remarried in 1983 after we had met with Pastor John and got our heads on straight. From that time on, we truly became one. I had believed from the day I first met Bob that God had sent him to me.

Bob was my fulfillment. I was Bob's fulfillment. We were true partners. We did practically everything together. We were even thinking alike. We had truly found that first love that had consumed us when we first met.

One day in 1992 Bob noticed a slight swelling on the front of his neck. I looked at it and felt it.

"If it doesn't go away, I think you should have a doctor check it," I told him.

A week or so passed and the swelling didn't go down. In fact, it seemed to be getting larger.

I went to the doctor with him. When he felt Bob's neck, the doctor said, "This isn't good. It's some kind of a tumor. We better do a biopsy . . . check it out. Make sure it isn't cancer."

Cancer? Bob might have cancer? No! He couldn't have! Not my Bob!

We got the biopsy result right after we gave an engagement party for Rich and Lisa, attended by 125 people.

CANCER!

We were numb.

It was cancer of his thyroid, which is considered to be curable, but not Bob's. His had been caused by exposure to large amounts of radiation. For years at his work he had sat with a 10- by 10-foot machine surrounding him on three sides that unbeknownst to Bob was putting out a large amount of radiation.

Bob and I decided to *live* with cancer. We weren't going to give up and feel sorry for ourselves. We were going to continue to do things we thought were important, but mainly to *live* each day.

We started by going out to dinner that very night at a restaurant in Hanover Park called Pipers. It was one of our favorites. The waitresses all knew us.

When the waitress took our orders, she asked what she could get us to start. I said, "A tall glass of red wine."

Bob said, "Me, too."

The waitress knew we didn't drink and said, "Are you kidding?"

I said, "It's no joke. Red wine, please."

She brought it and we drank it down. We called for the waitress and told her to bring each of us another glass of wine.

"Are you sure?" she asked.

"Yep. But don't look under the table, cause when I drink I usually get naked," I said.

That made her laugh.

The next day Bob told the girls in his office about his cancer. They cried, but he tried to reassure them.

"Look, I'm in a win-win situation. If I die, I get a new body. If I don't die, I get to remain here a little longer. Either way I win."

A week later we went back to the same restaurant and got the same waitress.

"Are you drinking again tonight?" she asked.

"No. We gave it up."

She said she just couldn't believe we drank two glasses of wine each the last time we were in. "Were you celebrating something?"

"No, not exactly," I said. "We had just found out that day that Bob has cancer."

Working side by side, we planted an English garden close to the downstairs windows so that, looking ahead, when Bob would no longer be able to walk, he would be able to look out the window at the flowers and herbs. We put a bench in the garden and added a playhouse that the kids had grown up with, which I had been saving for their children. The bench had belonged to his parents; Bob's boys, Robbie and Rusty, had cleaned and painted the frame and re-did the seat with newly stained wood. Bob loved it.

We had a terraced area for vegetables and an arbor with white lace flowers covering it. We added a pond and put in a fountain to add that very relaxing splashing sound.

We would walk about the yard, enjoying the colors and the scents of the beautiful flowers.

Bob had built a screened-in porch, where we would give afternoon lunches.

I packed the freezer full while we still had an income.

We sponsored an engagement party for my older son Richard, and Lisa, his bride to be. We had 125 people in our back yard. They were married a year later.

That very day we got a phone call from Bob's son Robbie, who was serving in Italy. He had found the girl of his dreams, Vicki, and would be getting married in a year, a week after Rich and Lisa.

Richard's mother-in-law gave him and Lisa a $40,000-plus wedding, which wasn't what the couple had wanted. It was the wedding Lisa's mother had always wanted for herself. The kids came close to running off, but the pastor talked them out of it.

Robbie's wedding, on the other hand, was a lie. They had already gotten married but wanted their parents to give them a reception. It was held in the American Legion hall with lots of homemade good food and fun, but it was on a shoestring budget.

A few years later, Rich and Lisa divorced. Not long after that, Robbie and Vicki divorced, after their son, Jonathan, was born.

Bob's other son, Rusty, married Dena after Bob died. After having sons Zackary and Anthony, they divorced.

Bob and I each had an operation a month before their wedding. He had a lung removed, and I had a hysterectomy. We were up and dancing for both weddings.

We went out dancing a lot, because that was what we liked to do.

His first doctor's appointment was with an endocrinologist. We told him right off, "Bob has cancer."

He said, "Nobody ever says he has cancer."

"Well, he does, and we want to know what you can do about it," I said.

"I don't know," he said.

"Well, when you do know, would you tell us, because we'd like to get rid of it," I said.

We had decided to be as open about the cancer as we could, without any hidden words or agendas.

This was the first of 44 doctors that Bob would see in the next five years. With some appointments we were told we'd have to wait three months. I would tell them if they had a cancellation to call us, and that we could be there in an hour. This happened several times.

His cancer spread from the thyroid to under his shoulder and grew like a big potato. Then it moved to a lung and then to his hips. He would later fall and break both of his hips on the same day. It moved into his bones, up his spine and back.

Doctors did surgery on Bob's throat three times. One time they severed a vocal cord. They removed the lower lobe of his right lung.

He early on began receiving radiation treatment daily.

We met many people undergoing cancer treatments that were far worse than Bob.

We met a woman in the hospital who came in daily with her husband. One day I was talking with her, and she said her husband was doing all the cooking, that he was not very good at it. I asked her if she could have any kind of food, what would it be? She said chicken noodle soup and egg custard.

The next day I made both dishes, packaged them to go, and brought them to the hospital. The woman's eyes lit up, and she couldn't stop saying thank-you.

I was anxious to hear how she liked both dishes, but she didn't come to the hospital on the following day. I asked the nurse, "What happened to Mrs. Benz?"

"She died yesterday," the nurse said. "Today is her funeral."

I was shocked. I knew she had looked weak, but not *that* weak. Her husband called a week later and asked me out to lunch to repay me for the two dishes. I asked Bob to go with me, but he said No, that I should go, that he wasn't feeling up to it.

As it turned out, neither was I. The man hit on me and told me that when Bob died, I could move in with him.

No thanks.

Bob lived for another two years. I never contacted that man again, nor did I ever offer chicken soup or custard to anyone again either. After I told my friends this story, they jokingly told me that when they're sick, please don't make them chicken soup.

After seeing all those doctors, having countless tests performed in three different hospitals, and undergoing more radiation that anyone could ever imagine, Bob died. His death came at home in June of 1997.

For a while Bob thought he was getting better and was making plans to go back to work. He had struggled so hard to walk again. But the cancer started spreading again.

I was taking him in daily for radiation, but the pain was so bad, he could no longer walk. I told him we would hire an ambulance to take him in, but he said, "No. I'm not going in for any more radiation. Call the hospice people."

The next day I called CNS Hospice on North Avenue in Carol Stream.

With hospice, I was surprised at how little time is spent with the patient -- approximately an hour a day. We thought the hospice would bring in a nurse to be with Bob throughout each day. Not true. A nurse came only three times a week, each time for about an hour's visit. A man came to bathe him twice a week and change his bedding. The rest of the time we were on our own.

I learned quickly that with hospice, you don't call 911 or you'll end up on machines.

Our doctor would call every evening at 5:30 to inquire how Bob was doing.

We had a hospital bed in our family room, along with a portable potty, and an oxygen mask with an extremely noisy mister. I built a screen to muffle the roar.

Bob would often tell me how grateful he was for all I was doing to make him comfortable.

Bob had been teaching a group of young men tool and die skills at Wisconsin Tool & Stamping Co., where he was employed. One day the men came to our home to visit Bob. Pulling into our driveway, the setting sun momentarily blinded the driver of the car, and their car accidentally struck another car in our driveway, causing minor damage.

They gave Bob the greatest gift of all. They thanked him for his training and shared with him what a wonderful boss he was to work for. They said they had been proud to undergo their training with Bob.

That was the day Bob's hospital bed was delivered. He had been losing weight at a rapid rate.

Shortly before he died, Bob sent me out to find a funeral home and cemetery. I asked Bob Karp, our neighbor, to remain with him while I was gone in case Bob needed help getting out of bed.

Bob wanted to die at home and said, "I'm going to speed things up."

I asked how he proposed to do that.

"I'm not going to eat, because when I do, I choke on the food anyway, and I don't want to die like that."

I said, "That all makes good sense, but I don't want to ever be accused of not feeding you. So I will cook daily -- make easy things for you to eat and offer them to you. If you say no, its your choice."

Bob had weighed 175 pounds at our first meeting 24 years ago. Now he was under 100 pounds.

He had me send invitations to the last 10 doctors he had seen -- an invitation to attend -- not his funeral -- but a *celebration of life*.

He had me contact Tom Johnston from our church to sing at his funeral. He requested that our pastor preach a salvation message. And that the pastor did, telling how Bob was not afraid to die -- that he knew Jesus as his savior.

The day Bob died, I was sitting on his right, Pastor John was sitting on his left, my sister Joyce and my friend Rhonda were standing at the foot of the bed talking. Mother, who was living with us, was upstairs.

I had been at other bedsides when people had died, but had seen nothing like what I was about to see. Pastor John had been at countless deathbeds and he said he had seen nothing like it.

All of a sudden we saw the flow of blood under Bob's skin wash up his shoulders, over the back of his head, over the top of his head, and come down his face, and wash out.

"He's gone," I said. "God just took him."

"Yes," Pastor John said. "I've never seen anything like it."

"Me either," I said.

Joyce said, "No, he's still breathing."

I said, "It will stop. He's gone. I just watched his spirit leave."

Before Bob died, he asked me to send his doctors a note to inform them he had died, to thank them for their excellent medical care, and to welcome them to attend his *Celebration of Life*. One of the doctors attended the service, and two sent me letters.

The invitation read:

Celebration of Life

Judith Neumann-Dicks

ROBERT E. NEUMANN

April 30, 1943
to
June 26, 1997

After a five-year battle, cancer has made it possible to be home with my Lord and Savior. We wish to express our appreciation for the excellent care you have provided.

Friends may call at
Rosedale Chapels,
450 W. Lake St.,
Roselle, Illinois,
Tuesday, July 1, 1997,
3 to 9 p.m.

Services will be at
Grace Community Bible Church,
6N171 Gary Ave.,
Roselle,
Wednesday, July 2, 1997
10 a.m.

Interment will be in
Bluff City Cemetery,
Elgin, Illinois

Eternal Home will be in
Heaven

For his funeral, to help me realize that this was to be his *celebration of life,* I decided to wear white. After all, it was truly a joyous event, because I knew Bob was finally home with the Lord.

There was no doubt in my mind that the Lord had carried us through those last five years while Bob fought his cancer.

The money had almost run out, and our daily needs had been met. All the doctors and hospitals got paid. There was even enough left over to cover the cost of flowers. Over 500 people came to the funeral.

Jacob flew in from San Francisco. Rich was by my side every step of the way.

For the next four weeks Pastor John preached every Sunday, bringing up Bob's death. I couldn't take it anymore.

At the service the next week while the singing was going on, I was having a silent talk with the Holy Spirit.

Do you want me to tell them?

Yes.

How about at the evening service when there are less people?

No.

But, Lord, I'm having a bad hair day.

So?

You'll have to make my feet move.

And he did.

I got up and touched Joyce's arm.

"Tell 'em, Jude."

Now, Lord, you told Joyce. Can't you tell the others?

Half way down the aisle, Carol, a friend, stepped out and touched my arm.

"Tell 'em, Jude."

Now, Lord, you told Carol. Why can't you tell 'em all?

That's your job.

But Lord, you know that women don't speak in this church.

Now I had reached the front pew. I stopped. Pastor John stepped aside. I went up and touched his arm. I wanted him to feel the Holy Spirit as I was feeling him. I faced the congregation and felt my mouth open and heard the words begin to come out.

"For four weeks now, Pastor John has preached on Bob Neumann's death. Let me introduce myself. I'm Judy Neumann, Bob's widow. I am here to tell you that Bob was just a man -- a man who knew the Lord and who was not afraid to die. He had accepted the Lord into his life at a young age. He had lived a godly life and is now rewarded with the gift of eternal life, of which Pastor John and I witnessed at his death.

"What I do know is that when Bob prayed, and when we prayed together, we got answers.

"If you are carrying any ill feelings or hate or unforgiveness toward anyone, give it up, because your prayers won't go any higher than the ceiling. God loves you just as he loves Bob, and he wants the very best for you. After all, he created us, and we are his children."

I stepped down, and three people stepped into the aisle and said, "That was for me."

I said, "Then it's time to do something about it."

Right about this time, I remember seeing Lori, who was a friend of my son, Richard. Lori had her new baby, Angela, with her. After Lori had gotten pregnant, her boyfriend, the expectant father, beat her and left her. I was prompted to write the following:

Fear

An unwed mother was filled with fear
Before her child's birth.
The birth took place a week ago;
How quickly it fades away.
She admires her child
And is amazed at your creation, Lord.
Those tiny little fingers,
A rose bud nose,
Dangling little legs and toes
Spread like ostrich plumes.
Her heart is filled with love, Lord.
Knock gently.

Chapter 22

Bob's Background

While Bob was battling cancer, this was the time in our lives when we were *closest to God*. We prayed together. I went with him to each doctor's appointment. Our Bible study group, called a "fellowship flock," met weekly in our home.

When people would come to our home to cheer us up, they would leave marveling at our sense of peace, at our sense of joy. They couldn't believe it.

It was during one of these moments feeling close to God that I wrote the following:

Peace

I'm in love with him above.
He's there day and night.
He takes away my fears
And soothes my tears;
Fills my head and heart with joy.

Peace is not just a word on a Christmas card.
Peace is homemade and found within.
He is there for you,
As well as for me.
Take off the blinders and you'll see.

Ask him in
and he will dwell with you
All the days of your life
And in your after-life as well.

It was two months later to the day when I received a card from Julie, the mother of Jim, who had been my husband number three. She wrote, "I want you to know that Jim died January 15, 1997. His cancer had returned."

I recalled the numerous deaths that besieged me in 1979. Would this be another 1979?

Two months later a friend, Sherry Snyder, phoned and asked if I'd like to go back to work, that she knew of a job for me. I took it. It was full-time work for a graphic arts company. I had been working for an insurance company and hated it.

Mother was living with me at the time, which helped a great deal. But it had been much too soon for me to go back to full-time work. I would cry on my way to and from work each day.

During one of those crying sessions I got to thinking about Bob's parents. Since Bob's father was also called Bob, to minimize confusion, I'll refer to Bob as *Bob Jr.*, and to his father as *Bob Sr.*

Bob Sr. and Helen had run off and got married. Helen's mother had died at an early age, leaving three daughters with an alcoholic father. That's how Helen happened to have a *glass eye*.

One night her father came home and made demands. When Helen, the oldest of the daughters who had inherited the household responsibilities when their mother died, didn't jump fast enough to suit him, he threw a hairbrush at her. It severely damaged her eye, causing her to lose it.

Helen was about five feet tall. By the time I met her, she was kind of round about her middle. She always wore dresses with a clean apron covering her large bosom. Her salt-and-pepper gray hair was almost always tied up on the back of her head. Although she wore glasses, one could still tell she had a glass eye.

She was a great cook and baker. She won my heart with her homemade dinner of pork roast and dumplings.

Helen and Bob Sr. married in Chicago at about the start of World War II. He was soon drafted and served in the Army, seeing action in Europe. He always declined to talk about his war experiences.

Bob Jr. was born in 1943, and his brother, John, in 1945.

Helen, as a young mother, was living in a Chicago apartment on Adams St. Her sisters were thrilled to help Helen with her sons, as were, it seems, everyone else in the neighborhood. Helen and her sister Irene, along with Irene's friend Gerry, worked at the time with the telephone company.

Helen used to love to tell the story of how one day she was doing some grocery shopping in her neighborhood, pushing Bob Jr. in a buggy. First she stopped at a little store and bought a pound of butter, which was rationed at that time. She placed the butter in the buggy alongside her sleeping son. Then she went to the meat market. Meanwhile, Bob Jr., unbeknownst to Helen, woke up and, while she was buying meat, ate the butter.

When Bob Sr. returned home from the Army, he joined the Chicago Police Department. He served as an officer for 30 years and had a number of commendations in his file when he retired.

Bob Sr. was tall and weighed about 175 pounds. Upon his retirement, he was balding with gray around the sides. He was still handsome and it was easy to surmise that he had been a ladies man in his younger days. I could readily see where Bob Jr. had got his good looks and sparkling eyes.

Bob Sr. loved to play with his sons and enjoyed helping them make and fly kites. He used to love to tell the story of how one day Bob Jr. got his kite in the air and had tied the end of the string around his little brother

Johnny's waist. The wind picked up suddenly, almost blowing Johnny away.

Bob Sr. was always the gentleman to Helen. Her pictures always had a prominent place in their home.

Bob Sr. and Helen and their sons lived only four blocks from my family when I was young and when Mother was working in the Chubby Dept. at Madigan's. That was when I first met Bob Sr. when, as a policeman, he served as a crossing guard at Delano School.

Bob Jr., who was chubby growing up, was involved in ROTC and band in high school. His brother John, always thin, got to be very good at baseball and likely would have played for the Chicago Cubs or White Sox had his girlfriend not discouraged him.

I didn't meet Bob Sr. and Helen until after he had retired from the Chicago Police Dept. and they had moved to Twin Lakes, Wisconsin. They were always so warm and friendly, greeting me with a gentle kiss and hug.

As the years passed, Bob Jr. and I were not close to his brother, John and to John's wife, Carol. Surely, that first day we met, when I had shut the door several times in their faces, had something to do with it. I can think of seeing them at only two Thanksgivings.

Helen used to say that John and Carol would come up to their house at Twin Lakes only to wash their car that they never offered to help out as did Bob Jr. and I. They would usually go visit Adell and her husband, John, while Bob Jr. and I helped out at the house. John and Carol liked going golfing, which was cheaper in Wisconsin.

While Bob Jr. was in his last two weeks of life, I suggested that he call his brother. He did, and John told him he was too busy to come see him, but that he would come to the funeral.

Why bother? I thought. "Don't come for *me*," I told him. "It's your *brother* who is reaching out to you."

After Bob Jr. died, John and Carol showed up. I almost wished they hadn't come. It was too little and too late.

But they were in church while Pastor John preached his salvation message as Bob Jr. had requested. Maybe there was a real reason for them to come. I hope so.

Chapter 23

Early Painful Memories

In a matter of a few days I would be turning thirty. I got to thinking. Nearly thirty years of my life had past, and I never had been able to say no to anyone. I had always allowed myself to be used and to be somewhat abused. I didn't speak up. I was a Christian, and I thought that's how Christians did things.

Why was I like that -- *a doormat?*

Was it the rape? No, I reasoned, because the rape had occurred when I was 27, and I was a doormat before that. No doubt that the rape severely damaged my self-image.

I began to relive the rape, remembering how I had fought with Roy all the way down the hallway, digging my nails into the woodwork saying, "No! No! No!" And how when we hit the bed, how I shut down. He might just as well have raped a dead person because I was mentally not there.

All I could think of was Please God don't let my boys hear all the commotion.

Superwoman doesn't live here anymore

I thought about Roy, how we had dated a few times and how I had told him on the phone I was going to marry. I'm sure that's what had made him so angry. He was feeling a deep rejection.

There's a saying, "What doesn't kill you makes you stronger." The rape didn't kill me. Was I, therefore, now stronger?

Yes!

I still hadn't told anyone about the rape except for that psychiatrist. It was still my deep, dark secret. Like a festering sore, it would eat away at my insides until I thought I absolutely couldn't take it anymore.

I was so ashamed at what had happened. Yet, I knew it wasn't my fault, that rape is an act of violence against women.

So, if the rape hadn't turned me into a doormat, what had? I thought about my early life.

Wait a minute. *There was something.* Way back when I was only four years old. I had kept *that* secret buried deep inside me all my life.

I had been *molested* several times by a relative, who told me, "Don't tell anyone. This is our secret."

Had that turned me into a doormat? How could it? I was only four. I didn't know anything. I didn't know I was being molested. How could something I truly didn't know about or understand turn me into a doormat?

Maybe it was something else early in my life. What about at the end of the first grade when the teacher met with Mom and they decided it would be best for me to repeat the first grade?

My heart began to pound. *That's it! That's it!*

It was my eyes. The teacher had finally discovered I couldn't see very well. I was sent to an eye doctor and fitted with glasses -- and held back to repeat the first grade.

That's it! That's it!

I felt myself blush; reliving the rejection I had felt then. I was a laughing stock in that second year of the first grade. I, after all, had been held back. I hadn't been smart enough to go on to the second grade with my original classmates.

In that second year in the first grade, I stood out. I was the tallest kid in the class. I couldn't hide my shame.

Not only was being taller than everyone else a source of my feelings of rejection, but my glasses added to it. My new classmates called me "four-eyes."

I remembered how I had decided to solve my dilemma. I would try harder to be liked by my new, younger classmates. I would bend over backward to please everyone. Yes, I would be liked. Yes, I would *please everyone*.

I could still feel my heart pounding. I was still blushing, reliving that pain of being held back. Reliving the anxiety of striving to always please everyone so I would be liked.

I began to cry, at first a quiet sobbing. This grew gradually into a choking sob, a paroxysm of pure pain. It was as though my insides were purging themselves of all that locked-in pain and rejection . . . and trying to please everyone.

No wonder I had for so many years been *Judy the doormat*. I had been trying to please everyone in order to escape the pain of more rejection.

That was it! That was when my striving to please everyone turned me into *Supergirl*, which, of course, later on grew up into *Superwoman*.

I became the woman who could do anything for anybody. You want something done? Just ask Judy. She'll do it.

I prayed about my dilemma. I knew I couldn't turn myself around by myself. I needed God.

Then it hit me. *I needed to forgive.* Forgive that person who had molested me when I was four. Forgive that teacher and my mom for making me repeat the first grade. Forgive Roy the rapist. *Yes, even forgive Roy the rapist.*

I remembered *Proverbs 22:6*. "Train up a child in the way he should go, and when he is old, he will not depart from it."

Mom had trained me well, taking me to church and Sunday school in my early years. And Mom's daily devotions and sharing in our home also built my character.

Sure, I had known failure back when I was held back in school. But there were a few bright spots. Because I was a year older than everyone else in my class, I was the fastest runner.

But now I was able to realize: this was not failure; this was empowerment, and I liked it!

Yes, I forgive that person who molested me when I was four. I will admit it was a relative who did it, but I will never reveal his name.

Yes, I forgive the teacher and Mom for holding me back in the first grade.

Yes, I forgive Roy the rapist.

A note to whoever reads my story, you had better forgive those who have hurt you. It says in the Bible, "If you don't forgive, God won't forgive."

I decided right then and there to place everything into God's hands. I leave everything up to God as to how he wants to handle things.

I had a lady friend who went to her deathbed hating her father for what he had done to her in her teens. I wouldn't want to be her. Forgiveness is very important for freedom in Christ.

I don't think I would feel the way I do if it hadn't been for Christ in my life. He is my heavenly father.

As I reflect back on my life, I see things more clearly than ever. Think of your life as consisting of little boxes, good and bad. Now put them into a square. Are there more good boxes than bad? Despite all that has happened in my life, I see many more good boxes than bad.

Although I grew up in a dysfunctional home, Mom managed to put *fun* into the word. We would have devotions together; we would play a game at the dinner table.

"Learn a word a day; use it in every way," Mom would say.

We would have a Ted Mack's Amateur Hour, performing whatever talent we thought we had. We had movies and popcorn at our house on Sunday afternoons. We also had great Sunday dinners.

My dad was not only very handsome, but was also smart and talented. His downfall was alcohol, which made him lack a sense of responsibility.

When I married David, I wanted a family just like ours: two boys and two girls. I didn't see that alcohol would wreck our marriage, just as alcohol destroyed my parents' marriage. They divorced after 25 years. When David and I divorced, I felt relieved that I wouldn't have to go through what my mother endured.

I remember feeling empowered when I left the courtroom after my divorce was granted. I recall humming the song with that famous line, "I can see clearly now the rain is gone." *I was free.* Not a worry in the world. I had a job managing a boutique. I had an apartment. But most of all I had my boys, the joy of my life. And, most important, I had God on my team. I knew I couldn't fail.

Sure, there had been disappointments in my life, but God had been there 24-7. I didn't have to worry; I would pray at night and turn my problems over to God. I slept well. God was up all night. Let him handle the big things.

Hadn't God supplied my needs? When I came back to the Chicago area from Washington, DC, God supplied an apartment, furniture, food, and a job. That was all I needed.

It wasn't long before I moved to Schaumburg for a better paying job that included my rent and all utilities. God was faithful, and so was I. Things were going well. I was dating; men were knocking at my door. And then I met Bob.

I didn't know it at the time, but I had some inherent talent in art and was even judged the best artist in my class and, along with my friend Vicki Logan, was awarded a scholarship for an art course at the Chicago Art Institute. And later on in high school, I would eventually catch up with the class from which I was held back. I graduated from high school in 3½ years.

It seems that art talent runs in our family: Mom, myself, Rich and Jacob (my sons), Al (my brother), Pat (Al's wife), Ward (Al and Pat's son), Katie (their daughter), Michael Hurley (my niece's husband), and Betty and Judi Gartrell (my cousins).

Printing talent also seems to run in the family, as evidenced by the following: Lester Steel (Mom's father), Ed Yokum (Mom's stepfather), Mabel Steel Yokum (my grandmother), Al Smith (my dad), and me.

Vicki and I had known each other since the fourth grade. We loved art and were in the same art classes in high school. We would work hard on our homework together. Vicki went on to art school and became a freelance artist.

Later, when I was married to David and moved with him to California, I got a job making view graphs, flip charts, and electrical schematics. My dream of working in the art field had come true. And the pay was good. I loved the work. But when David left for Viet Nam, I returned to Illinois, where I had another job waiting for me in a clothing store.

Thinking about Vicki Logan took me back to when I was eight years old attending James Monroe School in Chicago. We had moved to 2626 N. Kimball. Vicki lived on Diversey, right around the corner from Bonnie, who lived on Milwaukee Avenue. Bonnie's mother was a beautician, and she and her family went to Florida yearly. Bonnie, an only child, had beautiful hair, lovely clothes, and all the latest toys and dolls, including eight or 10 Madam Alexander dolls, each with a complete set of outfits. Back then those dolls sold for about $30 each. Nowadays they cost $150 per doll.

I thought of another reason to feel sorry for myself. I used to go home for lunch until one day I came home and my dad had been drinking and was sound asleep on the sofa. I decided from then on it wouldn't be safe to go home for lunch anymore, and I started eating at George's Pine Grill. I told my dad later that day that the reason I didn't come home for lunch was that I had been locked out and had eaten lunch at a neighbors. I never told him it was because he had been drinking.

At that restaurant, I would eat with a bunch of old, retired men, sitting with them at the bar. I'd eat a cheese-burger, grilled onions, fries, and drink a Coke with it every day. George, the owner, would demand money from the old guys when he felt they had enough coffee. He would say "Pay or go." They usually paid.

I would walk with Vicki, because it was just down the block from her house. I couldn't tell her mom the truth about why I was eating lunch at a restaurant. Dad was working on a night shift and would start drinking early in the morning.

When Vicki's mother, Eva Logan, heard I was eating lunch at a restaurant, she invited me to eat lunch every day with Vicki at her house. Vicki's dad was also an alcoholic. He seemed nice and he liked me. He worked days, and at 5:20 every afternoon, their dog, Clancy, would sit on the back of a chair at the window and wait for him.

Vicki had a younger brother, Dwayne. Bonnie started a club under her front porch and said it was for girls only. Vicki and I quit until Dwayne, Vicki's younger brother, could be a member of the club. Bonnie finally gave in and allowed Dwayne to join.

But it was a blow to Bonnie's ego. She had a temper and would storm off when she didn't get her way, calling out, "I quit."

Bonnie's family moved after the eighth grade to Morton Grove. We went there a few times to see her, but she had found new friends and didn't much want anything to do with us.

It's amazing how the mind works and what will trigger a past thought or experience. At the company where I was working, they were having a birthday celebration for a co-worker. As he opened the card, he shook it as if money would fall out. A light bulb clicked on, reminding me of how a woman friend Vicki and Dwayne's mother would send each of the three of us a Christmas card each year, with each card containing a dollar bill. The woman was single, had never married, and was very sweet. She thought we were the best-behaved kids in the world. Vicki, Dwayne, and I would always send her a thank-you card, mailed in separate envelopes.

One day sitting in Mrs. Logan's kitchen, the three of us got to thinking how when we mailed back the thank-you notes, we each had to buy a stamp, which would subtract from the value of the dollar. At first, stamps were only 10 cents, but gradually the price of stamps increased.

We thought: why not pool our money and buy a rubber stamp that would say: "Thanks for the buck, J.+V.+D.," and stamp a postcard every year. Of course, we were kidding, but Mrs. Logan was shocked we would even consider such a thing. Actually, we never did it, but it was fun thinking about it. Oh, by the way, when each of us turned 21, the dollar stopped.

Here's another fond memory: While my family attended the Irving Park Baptist Church, located at Kostner and Irving Park Rd. in Chicago, the church had a Baptist Youth Fellowship group. It was quite large, with chaperones. We would have a time for prayer and sharing. We would go on hayrides or tobogganing, ice-skating, roller-skating, and to bonfires.

That was the time in my life when I decided to turn my life over to Christ and be baptized. The baptism was done by full immersion on a Sunday evening in front of the entire congregation. Our church believed that when you were a baby, your parents would bring you in to be dedicated, and when you were old enough to make the decision on your own, you would be baptized.

It's funny how your young friends' names stick with you as the years go by. Other girls I used to run around with in that neighborhood included Judy, Alice, Nancy, and Kathy V.

One thing I remembered about Judy was that her dad had told her if she ever got pregnant before marriage, he would make her smoke a cigar. That was enough for her. She was very bright but quit school at 16 to get married. She had a son a year later and a set of twins at age 21. Her husband was killed riding a motorcycle, and Judy remarried.

Bonnie married an Italian from her neighbor and moved to Palatine. They had a boy and girl. When her parents died, she moved to Florida.

Vicki never married and bought the house next door. She worked for many years as a free-lance artist. She loved to play golf and travel.

Dwayne, Vicki's brother, married a girl from the suburbs. My goodness, but she had the biggest chest I ever saw. He later divorced and was living on the second floor of his mother's house. Victor, their father, died several years ago, and Dwayne died this year

I laugh when I think of Vicki's Auntie Ann. She never married. She didn't learn to drive until she was in her forties. One time she drove to the airport on a three-lane highway. She made it into four lanes in a white-knuckle ride. When she died, Dwayne moved into her apartment.

I used to live in their attic when I was married to David before we had children. Victor set up the cutest apartment for me.

Alice got married. They had a daughter, and she got a job as a buyer for Montgomery Ward. She later divorced and moved to Streamwood, a Chicago suburb.

I lost track of Kathy V. after the eighth grade. But I remember her telling us about when she got her first period. It became a topic of conversation at the family dinner table with her aunt and uncle and older brother present. I would have died in that situation.

Nancy went to a different high school, and we lost touch with her for many years. I last saw her at our grammar school's 25th reunion. She had moved to Wood Dale and had married. She hadn't changed; her hair and makeup were still perfect, just as it had been in her younger days. She was always very down-to-earth and a real sweetheart.

Sometimes, out of the clear blue sky, I would remember Larry, my first boyfriend -- that is, my first *serious* boyfriend. He was in the group of girls and boys I hung out with. We would go to socials at school and be together at parties. Larry went to Lane Tech, an all-boys' school, and I went to Carl Schurz. I was invited to his 16th birthday dinner.

My brother Ward called Larry *the creep*. He would ask me, "Are you still going out with the creep? Mr. Personality. Yeah, he has a *personality* all right, but he keeps it *hidden*."

Larry worked part-time at Woolworth's, and I was working for Maling Shoes. I was definitely in love. He for certain was going to be the man I would some day marry. So I thought anyway.

One day he came to me and said a girl at his work had asked him to take her to her prom, and he said he was going to do it. I was heart-broken. The record, "Judy's Turn to Cry," was popular then, and that is just what I did.

After this rejection, I went out on dates but didn't have my heart in it.

When Larry turned 16, he bought a car. One day we were on our way to a Lane Tech social. As we were driving down Kimball at Belmont, Larry decided to drag race another car. As soon as he took off, the police with lights and sirens came after us. Larry thought he could out-run them, and he did. He pulled into an alley, turned off the lights, and told me to duck as the police went by. Then we started out. But the cops got us anyway and issued Larry five tickets. They took me into another room and said they were going to charge me with contributing to the delinquency of a minor.

I said, "But I'm only 16. Call my mom if you have to. But I'd rather you didn't; I don't want to get charged with anything." They were trying to scare me, and they succeeded.

When Larry was going to court, he wanted me to go with him and lie. But I said, "No, I can't do that. I'll blush and turn red and they'll know I'm lying." I think that was the turning point in our relationship. As much as breaking up with Larry hurt at the time, Ward was right. It wouldn't have worked. He was a creep.

Oh, one more thing. When it came time for Larry to go to court, the arresting officer didn't show up. Larry's charges were dropped.

Some years later, after I had married Bob, I ran into Larry and his wife, Betty. They live over in the next suburb and have three boys. I liked Betty, and remembered her from school. But I was so glad things had happened the way they did.

But something was prompting me to realize that maybe God, after all, hadn't put me on earth to be walked on. So I decided, from that moment on, I was no longer going to be *Judy Doormat*. I was going to be *Judy Door*. With a door you can open it or close it as you want -- let things in your life happen or not happen.

Chapter 24
Daddy Dies

Main events have a way of etching a permanent place in one's memory. Among them is the death of a parent.

Daddy, as I called him for many years, died in November of 1979, on my son Richard's birthday. I was in my first marriage to Bob, and Bob's father had died in January of 1979.

I remember getting the phone call. Bob and I were returning home after a long day at Aunt Irene's (Bob's mother's sister). It was Thanksgiving Day. We had celebrated Richard's birthday. It was almost 9 o'clock in the evening when we walked into the house and the phone was ringing. It was Sandy, my sister-in-law, and my brother Ward's wife. At the time they were living in Wisconsin.

"Jude, I have bad news. Your dad died today."

I said, "How's Jill doing?" Jill was Sandy's sister and had come close to dying in a car when she was asphyxiated with carbon monoxide fumes.

Superwoman doesn't live here anymore

"Didn't you hear me?" Sandy said. *"I said your dad died today."*

"I heard you. I just don't know how to feel right now." I paused. "What happened?"

"He had a heart attack at the dinner table. Fell over and died."

My dad, Alfred (Al) Smith, was living with his second wife, Ruth, in Oshkosh, Wisconsin. She had been good for him but didn't want to share him with his four children.

Dad had retired in June of 1979, and they had gone to Hawaii to see the World War II memorials. He had been stationed there right after Pearl Harbor was attacked. That was his first time back.

Dad was in his forties when he and Mom split after 25 years of marriage. She just couldn't take his alcoholism any longer. Then he lived on his own for a number of years. He lived with his sister for a while, and he lived with my brother Ward in Florida. All this time he had continued drinking.

He moved to Wisconsin and lived with another sister, but this time he got a job. It wasn't that he couldn't work. It was just easier for him not to work and to drink.

Ruth worked for the same company, and that was how they met. She had been a foster parent for several mentally disabled men. They would go off to a school and be home for supper and sleep at her house. Dad didn't have a problem with this; he was very caring.

Dad stood tall and was very handsome. He had blue-black hair and a mustache, like in the comic books.

He was also very smart. He could read a book a day and had a great vocabulary. He also had a fine sense of humor. He dressed well and was super clean.

He was very talented in carpentry and quickly developed polish with almost everything he tried.

It was a shame he didn't take the time to learn about God. He never made room for God; he didn't have time for him. He lived his 65 years on his own terms.

He had never stopped loving Mom. Every time we talked on the phone, he would say, "Tell your mother I love her."

Because alcohol came first in his life, Dad was not very good at being there when you needed him. But I believe he truly loved all of us; he just couldn't give up alcohol.

His death hit me like a blow to the stomach. Now I'll never get to talk to him again, or even to say, "I love you, Daddy."

I had a nickname for him – "Pappa Doddles".

Dad had three sisters and three brothers:

Irene (Smith) Genze, Marietta (Smith) Young, Hilda (Smith) Grube, Robert (died at birth), Charles, and George.

Irene and her husband, Red, had a daughter, Tooty, and two sons: Bob and John.

Marietta and Chalmers Young didn't have children. It was a second marriage for Marietta.

Hilda and Frank Grube had two sons: Frank Jr. and Richard.

Charles and Phyllis Smith had a daughter, Valery, and two sons, whose names I don't remember.

George and Hilda Smith had a daughter and two sons. I just remember one son: George Jr.

I don't remember anything about my dad's parents, because they had died before I was born. I do know, however, that they are buried in a cemetery south of Irving Park Rd. on Narragansett in Chicago. When my dad's mother died, it was recorded as sleeping sickness. But I really think she had diabetes. She was overweight and slept a lot.

Hilda was very thin and had been sick for years. I wondered if she was diabetic.

Chapter 25
Len

After Bob's death, in June of 1997, I went back to work. It was probably the hardest year of my life. Mother was living with me in the big five-bedroom house. I had told her she could have any bedroom she wanted. She selected the largest bedroom on the second floor, the one closest to the bathroom.

Although I loved Mother dearly, and she was good company, it wasn't the same as having a loving husband living in the same house. I hated being without a husband and couldn't understand how Mother had done it for so long and still managed to be happy. I hated to go into a restaurant and see couples talking and enjoying each other's company. Would that ever be me again?

I remember attending a wedding in our church -- I had watched the bride grow up. I hated it when people asked me, "How are you doing?" I would answer with "Fine." What I really wanted to say was "My life is a mess, and I don't know if I'll survive. Every day I wake up for another day of hell."

To take my mind off grieving for Bob and cogitating about his five-year battle with cancer, I set out to work on the house. One of Bob's goals had been to make the house energy-efficient. He also had wanted to improve a number of safety features in and around the house, including changing the doors and locks.

The raised ranch house was big and beautiful. It had been built in the 1970s. It needed new windows and doors, and painting throughout to make it look fresh.

A curved sidewalk, which the neighborhood kids liked to walk on, made you think of the "yellow brick road." A large, handsome tree in the front yard had been planted 20 years earlier as a school project.

But God had other plans for me at this time of my life. And they weren't too shabby either.

For many years, I had been a garage-sale freak. I had learned that the best garage sales were in the better neighborhoods. Also, I got in the habit of checking out these neighborhoods for ideas on how to improve my own house and yard. I would collect future ideas regarding windows, sidewalks, shrubbery, and landscaping.

One of the better neighborhoods I liked to frequent was in the Kings Point Subdivision in Addison. About 15 years ago I was in Len's neighborhood, not knowing him. His best friend, who lived next door to him, was having a garage sale. I went to it and then drove around the neighborhood looking for landscaping ideas. I got a lot of them. When I went back home in Hanover Park, I hired cement workers to re-pour my front sidewalk. Then I planted boxwood bushes. They died, and I planted them again the next year, but they died again. Flowers went in the third year and lived.

I remember saying to myself a couple of times, Some day I'll live in a house like the ones I saw in that Kings Point Subdivision. God knew, but at the time I sure didn't know it would ever come to pass.

Before Bob died, he had been receiving care from Hospice of DuPage. After his death I began attending the hospice's grief-support meetings. I found them helpful, but perhaps a little bit "text bookish" on what to feel and how to feel it. The lady who taught the class had never had anyone she was close to die and consequently couldn't really relate to how it felt to lose a loved one.

In January of 1998, there were three men and five women attending the sessions, but as time went by, the number of men dwindled down to one, but the five women stayed. That one man was Len Dicks, whose wife of 42 years, Deloris, had died after a brief illness only one day before Bob had died.

Len suggested to me that we begin attending a different grief-support group that met at the hospital and was headed up by a pastor. We did change and found it to be more sympathetic.

One of the things we did in the sessions was to tell about the loved one we had just lost. Len spoke of his late wife as "Hon." He always spoke of her positively, never saying anything negative about her or about their relationship.

He was big-boned, 175 pounds, with a gray beard, slightly balding gray hair, and soft brown eyes. He had shattered his knee and walked with a cane. He looked about 60.

It was his idea to end each session with a hug. Why wouldn't he? After all, he was the only man. I watched him hug the other women and then when he hugged me, I couldn't help but notice that my hug lasted the longest. It made me feel so good, and being hugged by this big gentle giant made me feel little. But I was far from little -- I weighed in at about 160 pounds.

After this particular session, members of the group went out for some pie. Then Len took me out alone for some iced tea. As we were about to go our separate ways, I said, "Where's my hug?"

There we stood in the parking lot hugging.

After the eight-week grief-support course was over, I would see Len and other members of the group perhaps once a month.

Bob and I had enjoyed boating, and one day about a year after he died, I decided on a whim to use some of his life insurance money and buy a boat. I took my son Richard out to lunch to accompany me to take a look at a 23-foot cabin cruiser that was up for sale. I offered cash on the spot or no deal. Rich took me aside and told me I was offering only half the asking price. I said, "So, how badly do they want to sell?"

They accepted my offer. I now owned a boat. Call me *Captain Jude*. Now, with my boat, I went boating and dining almost every evening along the Fox River and up in the Chain of Lakes.

I had been working on the house practically nonstop for about a year. I had found a list of things that Bob had wanted to do. I did them all. I replaced the furnace and air-conditioner, installed new windows, doors, insulation, floors, new carpets, painted the kitchen cabinets, papered the walls, and added new furniture. I had the flowerbeds brimming over with flowers.

I decided to quit my job and throw a cookout party for my fellow workers. I remember the date: July 11, 1998, a Saturday. I invited Len. He decided not to attend the party because he wouldn't know anyone but said he would come after everyone left. He did and arrived at about 7 o'clock.

He came back the next day, Sunday, and we shared our lives and a bottle of wine on my screened-in porch. After telling him my life story, I figured if that wouldn't make him run and didn't make him have a heart attack, he was a good man. It turned out that it was his birthday that day.

I had been working for Glenhill Graphics as an office manager. I had worked for Sherry and Al many years earlier. They called and asked if I wanted the job. I had worked in the insurance industry before and was already in a job. But theirs sounded better.

A week later I took Len out on my boat, and the next day he took me out to dinner. The boat was moored at Port Edwards Rest on the Fox River at Route 62 and Route 31. We would go up through the locks and on into the Chain of Lakes. It was great on weekdays and nights, but not on weekends -- too many boaters.

Len and I started seeing each other regularly and on Oct. 8, 1998, God brought us together.

When you're living with someone, you can't help but learn lots of things about them. Some of the things I've learned about Len are: He's a retired electrician;

exercises daily; likes to read; favorite TV program is "The Price Is Right"; favorite color is blue; favorite cologne is Lagerfeld; loves to sing and dance.

My sister and her husband didn't live very far away in Hanover Park. After dinner they would often take a walk, passing right past my house. But they would never stop in. When Len and I had started dating, he would usually arrive at 8 o'clock, right after Joyce and her husband had walked past. They didn't know we were dating.

When I told Joyce that Len was in my life, she said, "Isn't this a little too soon after Bob's death?"

I replied, "For me or for you? No, I don't think it is too soon. Of course, you wouldn't know; you haven't walked a mile in my shoes."

If I had thought it was too soon, I wouldn't have done it. Len was living alone in a big, empty house, and so was I. We knew we would grow to love each other as time went by. But we were realistic; neither Len nor I expected that love to grow into the kind of love he had had with Deloris and the kind I had had with Bob. I was wrong, it did.

Early in Len's and my relationship, he invited me to meet his daughter, Michele, and her two daughters, Robyn and Leslie. At the time, Michele was in her early forties. She had dark hair; dark eyes, and was about 5 feet 2 inches tall, with a small build. She dressed well; I thought she was beautiful.

Robyn, Michele's taller daughter, looked very German. She was blonde with blue eyes and had a rather large frame. She was very pretty.

Leslie was a little shorter, medium-frame, with shoulder-length dark hair, and hazel eyes. She also was very pretty.

Steve, who was six-four, was Michele's husband. The girls took after him. They were a very handsome family, with two unruly dogs, a bird, and a turtle.

When I met them, I hugged each one, telling them I came from a long line of huggers. Our visit went well. That was the first time I had ever seen where Len lived. Surprise -- it was the house with the boxwoods.

Len invited me back to his house for steaks on the grill, and he made a tossed salad with garbanzo beans, which he called "Grampa Salad." It was his granddaughters' favorite.

Len had just reestablished his relationship with his daughter and granddaughters. They had been estranged for eight years. He missed them a lot and had missed out on the granddaughters growing up. Actually, he loved kids, and could really charm them when he dressed up in his Santa Claus costume. They would flock to him.

After that steak dinner, Len took me aside and asked, "In the grief-support group, you said you would never marry again. Why?"

I explained that Bob had left me with enough money to last me the rest of my days, that is, if I managed to prevent anyone from swindling me out of it.

Len said, "I think we were meant to be together. I felt it since day one. And, what if I have more money than you, then would you change your mind?"

The next thing he did was, take me to his laundry room. He said, "This is where I do my wash and where I fold my shorts and hang up my shirts."

I replied, "I think this is on a need-to-know basis, and I don't think I need to know."

We talked on, and I said, "I'm a package deal. My mother has been living with me for the last five years, and I'm not getting rid of her."

He said he and his little Yorkie dog, Scruffy, were a package deal too.

He gave me a blue sapphire engagement ring surrounded with diamonds, and we made a decision on October 8, 1998, that changed our single lives forever. We had an announcement printed up that read:

> God has allowed our paths to cross
> and our hearts to join as one.
> We would like to share our joy with family and friends.
> We were united on
> October the eighth, nineteen hundred and ninety eight.
>
> **Judith Neumann-Dicks**
> **and**
> **Leonard Dicks**

Please no gifts. (We sure could use your prayers.)

We sold my house and pooled equal amounts of money to get by on. In Len's house, I should say, our house, Mother ended up with a bedroom, a sitting room, and her own bathroom. She felt as if she had come full circle from the basement apartment of many years ago to this house, which she called the mansion.

And, Scruffy (the Yorkie) was a little doll. It wasn't long before she became my baby, and I loved her.

Len's house had a number of things I used to try to do at 1853 W. Laurel Ave. in Hanover Park: boxwood shrubs up both sides of the curved sidewalk, the rounded hedge in the back yard, and the hazelnut tree in the courtyard.

The inside of Len's house was another story. It wasn't my taste. Len gave me $25,000 to redecorate. I had a ball, and I used up only $12,000.

Oh, remember I was telling you Len and I changed grief-support groups? The group is still meeting once a month, but now, instead of meeting in the hospital, members are meeting in Len's and my house.

Since Len and I met, he has had two operations: one on a broken femur, and the other on a knee replacement.

Len's first wife didn't care much for travel, and it was something Len had always wanted to do. I love to travel, so our getting together was perfect. We've been three times to Florida, where we have two condos, a triplex (three apartments in one building), a duplex, and a single-family home.

Superwoman doesn't live here anymore

Here are other places we've been:

- Cruises to Alaska, Hawaii, Bahamas, and Mexico
- Virginia Beach for a reunion of the crew of a ship Len had served on in the Navy, taking in Laurel, Maryland, and Washington, DC; Connecticut; Branson, Missouri; Charleston, South Carolina; Jacksonville, Florida; and Baton Rouge, Louisiana
- Las Vegas to visit Len's friend
- Reno and Lake Tahoe for a wedding of the son of his best friend and next-door neighbor
- Yosemite and the coast of California, including the Hearst Castle, northern California where the redwoods are big enough to drive through
- Minnesota to visit Sandy and Ken.
- Puerto Vallarta, Mexico, for Len's nephew's wedding (We bought two time-shares and will be going back there. They can be traded in for any five-star hotel anywhere in the world. We plan to do that.)

We had planned to stay in Florida for three months early in 2009, but the trip turned into an adventure. See Chapter 34, "The Last Vacation."

While driving up the coast of California, we stayed one night at a brand new Best Western. The next morning driving out to a restaurant for breakfast, we passed a homeless man wearing a ski jacket and jeans that were torn all the way across the seat.

I said to Len, "Why don't we eat just half of our meals and put the rest in a box and find that man and give the food to him?"

We left the restaurant, and not seeing him, headed north to see the redwoods. When we got back, we drove around town looking for the homeless man but didn't see him. Then we stopped at a Laundromat. There was the homeless man sitting on the curb.

I went up to him and asked him if he would like some food we had gotten from a restaurant. He grunted, "Yes". I gave him the food, and he ate it so fast, as though he hadn't eaten in days.

As Len and I left the Laundromat, I said I wanted to go to a resale shop the next day and find some clothing for the man. We couldn't find any such shop. But as we were driving out to dinner, I spotted some tables alongside the road with clothes piled on top of them. It was a hospice group raising money with a huge garage sale.

I explained what I was looking for: a pair of jeans 32W by 36L. He showed me right where they were, and we made a donation

Len asked, "What if we don't see the homeless man again?"

Oh, ye of little faith!

We drove down the hill, and half a block away, there he was. Len stopped, and I got out of the car and handed the pants to the man, "Here," I said, "I thought you could use these."

He grunted again.

Superwoman doesn't live here anymore

We left town the next morning. I felt so good for having helped the man. I just couldn't look the other way and pretend not to see him.

Here are some activities Len and I are involved in:

- Greeters for the Addison Police Department court system. We greet people and direct them where to go.

- Members of CERT (Citizen Emergency Response Team), a FEMA organization. We help out during disasters, assisting people however we can. We recently helped with flood-relief.

- We both attended the Addison Senior Police Academy.

- The Addison Senior Club, which has over 200 members and meets weekly and stages outings and parties.

- Once a month we entertain men and women from Hines Veterans Hospital, taking them to the Addison VFW, where we cook and serve them a meal and play bingo with them.

- We both play Santa Claus for under-privileged children.
    - At Christmas we help deliver turkeys and Christmas trees to those in need.

- We are active at the Bloomingdale Church. Bob and I had belonged to Grace Community Church, but I thought it would be a good idea to change churches so people would not tend to compare Len with Bob.

- We pick up a friend for church each week.

- A grief support group still meets monthly at our house. It formerly met at Glen Oaks Hospital. We originally had 13 or 14 active members; now we have only six. People died off, moved, got married or went into a home. We now call ourselves "The Cake of the Month Club."

In addition, Len serves on the Addison Senior Commission. And I meet for lunch monthly with friends from Glenhill Graphics, where I used to work.

Len had been raised Catholic. Although he had not been to church in years, he told me he liked to sit in his back yard and talk to God, asking for his life to change. I was impressed.

Another pastime of mine: I helped out as a wedding coordinator at my church.

Len and I have great memories of the interesting people we meet in our volunteer work. For example, a young man named Daniel Hernandez worked with us at the Addison Police Department as part of his schooling. He was living in a foster home where he received a great amount of love. Daniel was in a wheelchair and had an attitude. He loved to talk sports. He would tell us what he did or where he went with his foster family. His foster father had taken him shopping and had bought matching outfits for Daniel and himself. Daniel even went with a date to the Senior Prom. Daniel died at age 18. As we watched a video of Daniel at his funeral, we marveled at all the living he had squeezed into his young life.

Remember, earlier I told you that Len didn't have a heart attack after I told him my life story? Well, he has a strong heart and strong arms. We're still in love after being together for over 10 years. Love is present every day.

It is indescribably beautiful to have each other to share our difficulties and joys. We were there for each other when his daughter went through cancer. We were there for each other when my son Richard went through "detox" and lived at a mission for a year.

We shared the joy of Len seeing his granddaughters finish college and complete their masters' degrees. Now both are going for their Ph.D.

Similarly, we shared the joy of seeing my son Jacob get married; his wife get pregnant with their second child, he was born in February of 2009; observe their daughter's first and second birthday; my son Richard get engaged to Mary. In addition, we were thrilled at seeing my stepsons (Bob's sons) Rob and Rusty, and Rob's son, who is 11; Rusty's two sons, by his first wife, and daughter, by his second wife.

Chapter 26

My Religious Beliefs

People often ask what religion I belong to. I am a Christian, a believer in Jesus. I don't belong to a cult or to an extremist group. I attend an evangelical church that believes in the Bible. I read the Bible to know the difference between what is real and what isn't.

I believe the Bible is the inspired word of God and that the people who wrote it were among his flock that he entrusted with what he was going to do for the world. He sent his son, Jesus, to walk the earth. All who believe in Jesus will have eternal life; those who don't will face eternal damnation.

I don't believe in a *hell on earth,* although I have met some people who would differ with me. Hell will come for those who do not accept the Lord.

Who is God? He is the almighty being who created the heavens and the earth. I believe that God created man (and woman) directly, that we did not evolve from apes or monkeys. I believe *evolution* is limited to changes within a species, that essentially, God created the various species of animal life.

God created man and took his bones to create woman, that we should have family. I believe God sent his son to walk among us and to sacrifice himself for our sin. I believe that Jesus hung and died on a cross, made from a tree that God had created. That on the third day, Easter Sunday, he rose again and ascended into heaven to be at the right hand of God.

When you see a newborn baby, how can you not believe in God? I believe by faith that God is real, that Jesus Christ is his son, and that when Jesus died he left his Holy Spirit to dwell within us.

I believe that God is with me at all times, that he is greater than all. I make a daily choice not to place other gods before me, such as money, drink, drugs, and various belongings.

I believe in God the Father, the father of Jesus Christ, and the Holy Spirit. I believe in a triune God: Father, Son, and Holy Spirit. I believe that the way to the Father is through the Son. I believe that if I will believe, I will be entitled to everlasting life.

I believe I am a King's kid, and I don't mind being a child of Royalty.

Chapter 27

Mother

By the time I was a teenager, Mom had had enough of Dad's drinking. He would get paid on Friday and be gone all weekend. By Monday there would be little money left from his payday.

When she went to court for her divorce, Dad was willing to pay $15 a week toward my support. The judge said, "Are you nuts? *Seventy-five dollars!*"

She had worked at Madigan's, an upper-class store on Madison St.

Now she was going to work full-time at Sauer's, a great German bakery. The owner was a woman in her fifties with gray hair and a personality just as sweet as her baked goods. Anna May, the owner's future daughter-in-law, had worked there at the same time as Mother. Mrs. Sauer, the owner, would bring cookies and milk to the back room. I would go there after school and do my homework and walk home with Mother on winter evenings, often in the snow.

I was 13 years old by the time Mom and Dad went through a divorce. We had moved to 2626 N. Kimball when I was 8 years old. It tore my heart out.

After my mother and father had divorced, she had lived with me, and then Gram.

She worked for Illinois Bell Telephone Company and changed jobs because of the late nights. This gave her telephone switchboard training and hence, more money.

She went to work in downtown Chicago for a group of lawyers. She was there only two months when she went for her divorce. One of the lawyers offered his services; he felt sorry for her.

But a month later she found out she needed a hysterectomy. After the operation she went back to work too soon and had a relapse.

Ward was home from the Air Force and was going to school to become an auto mechanic. Joyce was working full-time and dating Chuck, and she decided in July to announce that she was getting married in September.

Trouble seems to come all at once.

Next, Mother went in for a lumpectomy after a lump was found in a breast. She went into surgery not knowing whether or not she would have a breast when she woke up. But it was benign.

Ward and I wanted to cheer her up, so we painted and redecorated her bedroom to surprise her. But Joyce wrecked our surprise, telling her at the hospital what we had done.

When I was 13 years old, my sister, Joyce, and her husband, Chuck, had been living in a Chicago apartment located on Patterson. When they moved to a home in Hanover Park, mother and I took over their apartment. It was on an upper level of a house that had two bedrooms, a large living room, kitchen, and bath.

After I moved out, Gram moved in with Mother. But when Gram moved to California, Ward moved in with Mother after he returned from Africa and the Peace Corps.

Later, when Mother was alone, she moved into a one-bedroom apartment. We all pitched in to fix up the apartment. Sandy's brother installed green carpeting, Bob tiled the kitchen floor and changed the lighting, my son Rich plastered and painted throughout. Mother's landlord said he wished he had more tenants like Mother.

Mother was working full-time for the American Osteopathic Association and at the same time, taking care of her mother, and her sister, Phyllis.

When Mother was 42 years old, she was full of life. She took dancing lessons at Fred Astaire. She and her lady friend would go to Mattson's, a dance studio that would give a half hour dancing lesson before regular dancing would start. She had fun, the two of them going together. Mother felt there was safety in numbers. They would never separate and go home with a man, and there was no alcohol involved.

When I got married, Mother began dating a widower named Jim Coles, who lived in the same building. Just when their relationship was getting serious and they began to talk about marriage, Jim changed his mind. He made his decision after spending a weekend with his brother, who talked him out of it.

Mother was saddened, because she really cared for him. While she was dating him, her eyes took on a new spark, which had been missing for a long time.

I remember the day in 1984 when Bob and I had Mother and Jim over to our house for dinner, and Jim shared how after his wife had died, he had thought about killing himself. I wrote a short verse about him:

O, Lord, Doesn't the Devil Ever Rest?

> Lord, I met an old man on Christmas Day
> Who had wanted to take his life.
> This man had lost his wife.
> Didn't he know the gift was from you,
> The Gift of Life?

Sometime later Jim's health began to fail, and one of his brothers put him in a nursing home. Jim hated it, and after a short time, he had a stroke and died.

We then found Mother an apartment in Hanover Park that was close to three of her children. It was only four blocks from Bob and me, two blocks from Joyce and Chuck, and three blocks from Ward.

Mother had always had a great sense of humor, but lately she seemed to be feeling sad. The three of us tried to put some fun into her life. Now, with her living so close to us, we could take her to church and to Bible study. And much to Mother's delight, she found some church ladies to go shopping with and Myrldean Leone to go out to lunch with.

It was about a year or two after Bob and I found out about his cancer that Mother started showing signs of old age. She began to have difficulty opening jars, and also, she was getting to be forgetful. Bob and I owned a five-bedroom house, and there was plenty of room. I think it was really God's plan when we had her move in with us.

She was a big help to me. In fact, she was a real joy in my life. We didn't get in each other's way. I could really get her to laugh, and gradually the wall of strength she had built around herself came down. She had made it in this world and had survived without a formal education, and was still loved and needed. I really did need her.

Mother stayed home alone at first, but as time went by, we could no longer leave her on her own.

One day I took Mother shopping at Carson's. She was in the clothing section, and I went off to housewares. When I returned for her, she was nowhere to be found. I checked everywhere I could think of: the fitting rooms, the parking lot, and the washrooms. Finally I asked for help. I described her as being blonde, 5 feet 2, 125 to 130 pounds, wearing a turquoise jacket and jeans.

And wouldn't you know it? Of all the days in time, there was another lady in the store exactly fitting Mother's description: blonde, small framed, same jacket, and jeans.

I finally found her. She was trying on clothes in a fitting room and hadn't heard me calling for her. That was the day I woke up to realize that there is something wrong here. It wasn't long before we went to the doctor to see just what was wrong. He gave her a test and decided that Alzheimer's had set in.

He put her on medication to slow down the Alzheimer's development. That worked for about three years. I have to admit she was a darn sight better off than what I saw in a friend, whom I called Aunt Gerry, go through. Mother would pray to the Lord: "Don't let me lose my mind and don't let me be a burden to anyone."

When I heard the word Alzheimer's mentioned, I became deathly worried. The wife of one of our Seniors Club friends had the worst case of Alzheimer's I've ever seen. She couldn't talk, recognize anyone, or walk. All she could do was lie in bed. Would Mother get like that?

One night a few years later after Bob had died and she was living with Len and me, she got up to use the bathroom. Len was in the kitchen and I was downstairs reading. On her way back she got confused and went into our bedroom and got into Len's side of the bed and went to sleep. Len came downstairs to tell me Mother had gotten in our bed. I went up and woke her and explained that she had gotten into the wrong room and the wrong bed. She laughed and said, "I suppose you want your bed back. I'll change rooms."

The doctor said she had what was called *sundowners*. When the sun went down, confusion set in.

Having lived in Chicago for many years, Mother knew all about prowlers and break-ins. Consequently, whenever Len or I would leave the house, Mother would lock all the doors. Even when we would go out to work in the garden, she would lock us out. We had to carry a house key with us at all times, even if we went to take out the garbage.

As Mother was growing older and becoming increasingly forgetful, her tendency to be always locking the house, assured Len and I that we never had to worry about her wandering off.

Ward came and stayed with her while Len and I went on a cruise. We asked Joyce if she could come and stay with Mother, but she said she would stay with her but would rather do it in her own home. This happened I believe on three separate occasions. Mother did not do well with change.

Mother had developed heart problems and had been in the hospital several times. Each time, it seemed, Mother would exhibit a growing forgetfulness.

She had said a number of times, "I think I'm losing my mind." She would sometimes repeat the same question multiple times.

Mother, of course, moved in with us. She loved Scruffy (Len's Yorkie). When Scruffy died of kidney failure, Len, Mom, and I were devastated.

Len and I would take Mother with us every week to the Addison Seniors Club meeting at the Park District building. She loved it and made friends readily.

The Seniors Club would have lots of outings to the theater and to dinners. She loved getting dressed up and going out. I think she really enjoyed life with Len and me.

Mother liked to dress well, and she loved to shop. She and her friend would shop on Wednesday and then go out to lunch. I jokingly called it *the many happy returns,* because they usually returned one item less than what they purchased the week before.

Len and I quickly learned never to argue with Mother, but just let her win, no matter what. In her mind she was always right. What good would it do to argue with her?

Mother on occasion would walk around in her sleep. I am a light sleeper and would usually hear her when she was up. Sometimes when she would really be confused, I would make her a cup of hot chocolate (sugar-free) and sit and talk with her in the middle of the night.

I have a very calm voice and wouldn't question her but would talk about things that would take her mind off the moment. And I had a way of being able to make her laugh.

My son Richard would stay with Mother when Len and I would go away. Richard would make her feel like a queen. He would take her out to dinner and then thank her for the date. Jacob, my other son would send her flowers from Colorado every Christmas, Easter, and Mother's Day. He sent one bouquet for Mother, and one bouquet for me.

Both Bob and I, and then Len and I, would often take Mother with us to weddings and to other family events.

One of Mother's granddaughters has a husband named Dave, who was so cute with Mother at a wedding. He asked her to dance, and she said, "Oh, honey, it's too fast for me."

In her younger days Mother loved to dance -- fast or slow. Dave came by a little later and asked her to dance again and said, "Is this slow enough?"

"No" Mother said.

Pretty soon Dave comes around again, this time dancing with his wife, flopping her around like a rag doll. David said to Mother, "This could be you."

The next song was very slow, and Dave came around and again asked her to dance. This time she got up and started dancing with him. She felt like a queen, doing what she loves to do.

Dave Bulger, you'll get stars in your heavenly crown for dancing with Mom that day. She loved you.

Len and I fixed up a sitting room for Mother. We put a TV and a reclining chair in it so she could rest and elevate her legs. She learned how to work it and when she got tired, we would often find her in it asleep.

I had warned Joyce not to argue with her, but when Mother would go to Joyce's house to stay for a while, Joyce apparently would forget and argue with Mother. One time when Mother came back to Len and me after staying with Joyce, Mother was as mad as a hornet. She and Joyce had been arguing over shopping.

When Mother would go to Joyce's house for a short stay, she would take her own soap, shampoo, and toilet paper. Change wasn't good. Even after she got there, the arrangement of the bedroom and bath would confuse her at night. She wouldn't be able to find things packed in her suitcase.

She was doing basically all right -- she could bathe herself daily, clean her room, make her own breakfast, get dressed, and do her own laundry. She always had her makeup on and her hair fixed. And she always dressed well.

Paying bills, reading, remembering, and making a meal were the hard things for her. Change of any kind befuddled her.

Mother started getting days and nights confused and began staying up at night. When she was up, I was up because I didn't want her falling down the stairs. When I would try to catch a little sleep during the day, she would seek me out and wake me. I would get so exhausted I thought I was going to have a heart attack and die -- and Mother would be all right.

Finally, one day when I went with Mother to see a doctor, he recommended I should start looking for a nursing home for her. But I really didn't want to do that.

Not long after that, one day she slipped in the bathroom, and I thought she might have broken a rib. I had an ambulance take her to the hospital to get her checked out. They admitted her for observation, and I went home.

A little bit later the hospital phoned and said Mother was confused and wouldn't quiet down. I went back and explained to her that she had to remain there all night to have tests in the morning. I explained that if I took her home, Medicare would not pay the bill.

I told Mother we would pray about it. Several nurses joined us. I remember telling her I was going to pray to the same God she had taught me to pray to. This was my prayer: "Dear Lord Jesus, comfort Mother. Send your angels and bring peace to this hospital and to this room in the Name of Jesus."

By the time I was finished, she was sound asleep. Jesus had answered my prayer. The nurses said they had never seen anything like it.

There is power in the name of Jesus. It wasn't my doing; it was his. I stayed with her that night. She didn't wake up until morning.

I spoke with her doctor that morning, and once again he recommended we find a nursing home. He said we had 30 days to do it in, and that Medicare would pick up the first 100 days if she showed improvement.

I found a nursing home close to home that was not very modern looking, but it was family-owned, clean, and smelled good. I met several people in the hallways who had good things to say about it. The staff was almost all part-time, and they didn't look over-worked and burned out.

When I told Mother I had found a place for her, I expected to have a fight on my hands. I prayed first and asked God to prepare her.

I said, "Mom, it has come to the time when we need to look into a home for you. You require 24-7 care, and I just can't do it. We need help at night because you are not sleeping at night, and I'm not sleeping in the day."

She replied, "Okay, if you think so. I trust your opinion, and I know you have my best interest at heart."

She dressed up, putting on her red hat that she loved.

I remember the day I took her to the nursing home -- February 1, 2005. The director met with us and showed Mother around and took her to her room. Her roommate was a pushy person who had not apparently learned to share. She was so negative, that I wondered how this would work.

After leaving Mother there, at first I thought about not going to visit her for a while so she would be more dependent on the nursing home than on me. But I missed her and quickly changed my mind and went to see her daily.

She had adjusted better than I had thought she would. Mother didn't like her bossy roommate. Neither did I.

After visiting her for seven days in a row, on the eighth day when I arrived, she was sleeping in a chair. I stayed for an hour, waiting for her to wake up. I kissed her forehead and left.

The next morning I got a call from the nursing home asking me if they could send Mother to the hospital, that they couldn't get her to wake up. I said sure, I would meet the ambulance at the hospital, and perhaps she would wake up for me because she was so used to hearing my voice.

I called Joyce, and she and Chuck came to the hospital when the ambulance arrived and joined Len and me. As soon as we saw her, we knew her life was about to end. It was only eight days after she had been admitted to the nursing home. She had had a massive stroke. The nurse told us that most people her age take about three days to "bleed out." Looking at Mother, we knew it was just a matter of time.

We had her moved to a hospice unit. Len and I went to the nursing home and cleared out her belongings. We told them we didn't think she would be with us very much longer.

The next day we went back to see her, and I whispered in her ear, "I love you, Mom. Thank you for being a wonderful mother. We know you don't have to hang on for us. It's time, and if Jesus is there, reach out and take his hand."

Our pastor walked in on my little farewell utterance.

Len and I left to pick up my brother Ward, who was returning home from Mexico. Joyce and I called Al to let him know what was happening.

The hospital phoned us at 3:15 a.m., informing us Mother had taken a turn for the worse. I phoned Joyce and woke Ward. Shortly thereafter the hospital phoned again. Mother had died.

I thanked the Lord for not letting her linger. I could picture a party going on in heaven. After living almost 88 years, Bonnie was home. I used to kid her and tell her that when she got to heaven, she would get a crown with a jewel for each kind act she did here on earth that she hadn't been thanked for. God supplies the *Thank you.*

We had playfully nicknamed Mother the *Jell-O Queen*. She could make the best Jell-O salad ever. I had told her she would receive heavenly *jigglers* (flat pieces of Jell-O made on a cookie sheet).

Superwoman doesn't live here anymore

At the family reunion in 2008, we came up with a treasure chest of Mother's. It had a gold dollar for each grandchild, Jell-O boxes, and shopping bags -- all remembrances of Mother.

I had also nicknamed Mother *The Bag Lady.* She always seemed to be toting a bag of something or other. There seemed to be folded shopping bags everywhere.

I had no desire to go immediately to the hospital to view my dead mother. That could wait until well after daylight.

My head was filled with happier times and great memories. I knew I had had a hand in making her life happy. I had no regrets.

Mother didn't have any earthly riches to leave her children. But what she did leave us was priceless: the Lord to call upon and to serve as a guide through life's challenges.

I went back to sleep but was awakened by a phone call from the hospital's chaplain.

"Where are you?" She asked.

I tried to collect my thoughts.

"I'm home in bed. I was asleep."

"Why aren't you here?" She asked.

My brain was beginning to clear.

"I didn't see any reason to go out in the middle of the night to look at a dead body. Perhaps I should explain. My mother and I had a great relationship. She had lived with us for the last 12 years. The fact that she died is a gift from God. She doesn't have to live in that body anymore. As a Christian, I believe she is absent from her body and present with the Lord.

"So, you see, she is already in heaven -- in the twinkle of an eye. That's what the Bible taught me."

"Well," she replied, "there are papers to be signed."

"Can't that wait until morning?"

"Oh, I'm sure it can."

"I'll be there at eight o'clock to sign them."

I wondered why the chaplain had prejudged me. She apparently had thought I was the worse daughter ever. I thought, let's leave that up to God.

I was at the hospital at 8 o'clock. There were no papers; I had signed them the day she was admitted to hospice.

We had Mother's funeral on Valentine's Day, 2005. The date seemed so appropriate. We were burying our sweetheart that day.

Mother had left a letter she had written in 2000 after a funeral we both had attended. It was to be read at her funeral. Len read it. The letter follows:

My Dearest Children,

I write this with love in my heart for each of you, for you have given me great joy.

Superwoman doesn't live here anymore

Many years ago when your father and I moved to Chicago, we found a new life together. It was Gram and Ed who found Garfield Baptist Church, while your dad was in the Navy. I went back to church. It was there that Jesus came into my life. My own father was killed, and I had been so alone, with your dad gone. My heart was ready, the pastor prayed with me, and I prayed to God. I asked Him into my heart. I started reading the Bible and couldn't stop. I didn't know how easy it was until I prayed. When I read Jesus died for my sin, I knew it was true.

When you were little, I took you to church, and as you grew up, I prayed you would seek the Lord with all your heart.

I am so proud of all of you. You each have love for others, compassion, and the ability to forgive.

Al, if there were an award for being the greatest father, you would win hands down. You are a gifted writer (I enjoyed your cards) and wonderful teacher.

Ward, you have been there for me so many times. You have been my adventurer, world traveler, and even serving in Africa to help those in need. Your heart is so big when it comes to compassion.

Joyce, you are my missionary. You studied the Word and have witnessed too many. With the neighborhood Bible study and all the things you and Judy got involved in. Your mission field is here, keep on keeping on.

Judy has also been the adventurous one and has seen the beauty that God has created in this world. I thank her for all she has done in my life, and for all the care she has given so willingly. Yes, she is my worker.

This letter I leave with you because I am on a trip of a lifetime. Jesus promised me 66 years ago He would let me in His heaven. He gave me eternal life when I asked Him into my life. Teach your children and grandchildren, and I'll see you all again.

Yes, I arrived, and it is beautiful. More than anyone can imagine.

See you soon.

*Love,
(Signed) Mother*

*P.S.
Gram, Barb, and Bob send their love.*

*P.S.S.
Judy was wrong. My crown isn't made of jigglers.*

*P.S.S.S.
It took 2000 years to build all this. Wait till you see the place. Wow!*

Len almost choked up several times reading the letter. He doesn't like public speaking; but he did it for Mother. He really liked her. No way could I have read it.

The following is the memorial we had printed up for Mother's funeral:

Cover:

*"Well done, thou good and faithful servant . . .
Enter thou into the joy of thy Lord."
Matthew 25:21*

Superwoman doesn't live here anymore

Inside:

A Celebration of Life
For
Bonnagene Faye Smith
March of 1917 -- February of 2005

Opening Prayer
Pastor David Riemenschneider

Amazing Grace
(Congregation sings)

*Amazing Grace! How sweet the sound
That saved a wretch like me!
I once was lost but now am found,
Was blind but now I see!*

*Through many dangers, toils, and snares
I have already come;
His grace has brought me safe so far,
His grace will lead me home.*

*When we've been there ten thousand years,
Bright shining as the sun,
We've no less days to sing God's praise
Than when we first begun.*

The Lord's Prayer
Thomas Johnston

An Intimate Love Letter from Father God to You

Message
Pastor David Sunday

Judith Neumann-Dicks

The Old Rugged Cross
Thomas Johnston

It Is Well with My Soul
(Congregation sings)

When peace like a river attendeth my way,
When sorrows like sea billows roll;
What ever my lot. Thou has taught me to say,
It is well, it is well with my soul.

Refrain

It is well (It is well) with my soul (with my soul),
It is well, it is well with my soul.

My sin -- O, the bliss of this glorious thought,
My sin -- not in part but the whole,
Is nailed to the cross and I bear it no more,
Praise the Lord, praise the Lord, O my soul!

Refrain

And, Lord, haste the day when the faith shall be sight,
The clouds be rolled back as a scroll,
The trumpet shall sound and the Lord shall descend,
Even so -- it is well with my soul.

Refrain

Letter from Bonnie to Her Family
(Read by Leonard Dicks)

How Great Thou Art
(Congregation Sings)

Superwoman doesn't live here anymore

O Lord my God, when I in awesome wonder
Consider all the works thy hand hath made,
I see the stars, I hear the rolling thunder,
Thy pow'r throughout the universe displayed

Refrain

Then sings my soul, my Savior God, to thee,
How great Thou art! How great thou art!
Then sings my soul, my Savior God to thee,
How great thou art! How great thou art!

But when I think that God, his Son not sparing,
Sent him to die, I scarce can take it in
Then on the cross my burden gladly bearing
He bled and died to take away my sin

Refrain

When Christ shall come with shouts of acclamation
And take me home, what joy shall fill my heart!
Then I shall bow in humble adoration
And there proclaim: "My God, how great thou art!"

Refrain

Burial
Bluff City Cemetery
Elgin, Illinois

Luncheon
Chandler's Banquets
419 N. Roselle Road
Schaumburg, IL 60194

In addition to this beautiful funeral program, we also played a CD at the service that Mother had liked. Len had received a CD from my son Richard, and one Sunday afternoon I played it for her. She loved it and said, "Play that at my funeral."

The name of the CD is "An Intimate Love Letter from Father God to You." Various Bible verses are read aloud on it -- about how each of us is formed and how God knows our path before we are even born.

When Mother was still working, she had gone to the eye doctor because she was bumping into things. During an eye exam, it was discovered that she was blind in one eye. It was her prayer that she would never go blind.

Later she had a cataract on the good eye. She went in to have it removed, and when she came home and it healed, she looked in the mirror and said, "Oh, my God! My hair is gray; I thought it was blonde. People will be shocked."

I said, "What are you talking about, Mom? You have been gray for a long time. No one but you will be shocked."

I reflected on Mother's life, what she went through, and the parallels with mine. She turned a difficult life into something beautiful. I prayed that I might do the same.

One day near the end of her life, Mother came to me and said, "I feel like I'm losing my mind."

I said, "Well, Mom, I don't know whether or not you're losing it, but you have 87 years of information stored up there."

I gradually realized that the mind is like a computer: It stores information until you purge it out. This book is clearing out my mental computer, and I expect it will considerably lighten my load.

Chapter 28

Miracles

Yes, I believe in miracles! I should. After all, I have personally witnessed four of them: 1) my son Jacob's eye 2) Bob's hand 3) my arthritis (or lupus) 4) my grandmother's foot.

First miracle -- my son Jacob's eye

When Jacob was about 2½ years old, and we were living in the "pink house" (the house from hell), he developed a tumor on his eyelid in the corner of his left eye. A doctor at Great Lakes Hospital looked at it and then removed it with a scalpel.

Two weeks went by and it grew back, but this time in the middle of his eyelid. We took him back to Great Lakes Hospital. Little Jacob was terribly frightened and even traumatic as the doctor removed it.

Two weeks later it was back, this time in the corner of his eye next to his nose. We took him back to Great Lakes, and we told the doctor we wanted Jacob put to sleep while it was removed. The removal was scheduled for the following week.

My sister Joyce later asked me if I had prayed to ask the Lord to heal Jacob.

"No, the Lord has more important things to take care of. This is just a little tumor."

"Nothing is too little for the Lord," Joyce said, "He cares about tumors, both large and small. After all, he knows the number of hairs on our heads."

Joyce prayed, and then I prayed over Jacob.

The day we were to take him back to Great Lakes for the surgery, as I was drying him after his bath, I looked for the tumor. I looked again. *The tumor was gone!*

"Thank-you, Lord!"

I picked up Jacob and said, "Honey, we don't have to go to the hospital."

"I'm not going to the hospital," he said. "Those people hurt me, and I'm not going."

I called the hospital and told the girl who answered the phone, "Jesus healed my son's tumor, and we won't be there today."

She said, "It's about time he got credit for something. I'll tell the doctor."

I often wonder what would have happened if Joyce hadn't prompted me to pray over Jacob for a healing. How many more trips to Great Lakes would we have made?

Surely it was originally Joyce's faith, and then mine, that led to God's working this miracle.

Second miracle -- Bob's hand

One day after Bob and I were divorced, he called me and said to stop by the house, that he had some money for me. It was part of our divorce settlement.

When I got there, Bob was standing in the front hall with a bandage on his left hand that looked like an oven mitt, only white.

"What happened?" I asked.

"I cut it on a piece of steel at work. I just got home from the clinic. They stitched it up and now it's throbbing like crazy."

I suggested we pray about it.

I want to slip in a little confession here. I was still in love with Bob, and I hated to see him hurt.

We joined hands and prayed for Jesus to heal him and to stop the throbbing so he could sleep. He was due back at the clinic the next afternoon to have the dressing changed.

At the clinic when the nurse removed the bandage, *she could not believe what she saw.* The cut, which extended from his wrist for about 3½ inches to between his thumb and index finger, was *healed!* Hair-like stitches were sticking out of the edges of the healed wound. The nurse called in the doctor to see it.

"When did you do this?" the doctor asked.

"Yesterday," Bob said.

Bob asked the doctor if he could pull out the stitches because they itched.

"Sure," the doctor said. "I can't understand how the skin could grow together in less than twenty-four hours."

Bob told him about our prayer and said Jesus had healed it.

I got to thinking about God using me as an instrument in his healings. The healings were always for someone I loved. Perhaps this is what in every instance caused me to pray without ceasing.

The next day at work, Bob showed his healed cut to anyone who would look. No one could believe it.

Third miracle -- my arthritis (or lupus)

It was 1979. I was 33 years old. I was besieged with pain in my hands, feet, and lower back, making it difficult to stand and sing during Sunday services. My lower back hurt when I sat up, and my feet were turning in, as if I was starting to walk on the sides of my feet.

I said, "Lord, kill me now; please don't leave me in this body. I'm going to wind up in a wheelchair for the rest of my days."

The doctor said I had either crippling rheumatoid arthritis or lupus. He told me to go home and get a better insurance policy -- I was going to need it. He said he would hold off on more tests for two weeks so I could take care of the insurance.

He pointed out the knobs that had already formed on my hands. My father had suffered with arthritis, and his mother also. Her arthritis was so bad, she had to be carried around and had to hire help to raise her seven children.

I felt as though the doctor had just given me a death sentence.

The smallest task, such as writing, using scissors, opening a jar, carrying groceries in from the store, became almost impossible. I felt helpless.

I called a friend in the insurance business who said I could get a million dollars worth of coverage for $80 a month. I told him to send me the papers and I would fill them out and return them.

I didn't understand why I had this terrible affliction. I prayed and asked God to show me for what purpose he would allow this to happen. I knew God hadn't caused it; he was allowing it.

Bob was working late on this particular night, and I was sharing my problems with my son Jacob. We cried together. He said he would pray.

As I was praying, I thought of a 53-year-old woman who had lived in one of the apartments I used to manage. After suffering with crippling arthritis for 25 years, she couldn't use her hands or feet and was confined to a wheelchair and died.

I pleaded with the Lord. "You promised me you would not give me more than I could handle. Lord, I can't handle this."

When Bob came home, we prayed together. My son Richard stopped by in the morning. In telling him about my predicament, I broke down again. He said, "Why would God let this happen to a good person?"

I explained that he was not the *cause,* but that he was *allowing* it to happen, that there had to be a reason.

I called Lola, our church secretary, who came over to the house to comfort me. She knew I was more than just upset.

On Sunday I went to church with Bob, and I asked Pastor John Sale and the elders to pray over me. We were then attending the Keeneyville Bible Church.

I had read in the Bible that this is what's supposed to happen when one becomes sick.

The Lord had allowed miracles in my life before -- Jacob's eye and Bob's hand. And I knew I was brimming over with faith. I was certain I had enough faith to move even the Mount of Olives.

Monday went by with no word from either the pastor or the elders. Tuesday went by. By this time I was hurting badly and having my own pity party -- minus the hats and banners. Little did I know it was God's timing and not mine.

On Wednesday the pastor called and said they would pray with me right after the Wednesday night prayer meeting.

I figured my request was probably the first they had ever had. But that's what the Bible says to do: ask the elders of the church to pray over the sick person.

I was feeling sick to my stomach from the pills the doctor had prescribed. The enemy was trying to keep me home but didn't succeed. I went to the church and met with the elders.

We gathered in the kitchen, and all the elders spent time in prayer to cleanse themselves first.

A Bible verse came to me: "It didn't matter the measure of faith. The only thing that mattered was that we were praying to the same God."

The pastor asked the elders to examine their hearts and to pray for the removal of anything that might hold them back from praying over me properly. Then when they laid hands on me and started to pray, one man said, "Lord, heal Judy because she has done so much for our church."

I spoke out and said, "No, it's not about me. It's about what God can do."

They continued to pray, leaving me out of it.

The next morning I woke up to sleet, snow, and rain, and I had expected my pain to be compounded. The pain had a tendency to increase with a rise in humidity.

I called the church office, and the assistant pastor answered.

"See that weather outside," I said.

"Yes. Isn't it awful?" He said.

"Not here," I said. "I've got sunshine in the house. My fingers are straight. My feet are straight, and my back doesn't hurt."

Praise the Lord, I'm healed.

I went back to the doctor and showed him how I had been healed. I went to Pastor John Sale and told him how I had been healed.

"This isn't the first time I've witnessed a healing," he said.

I explained to him how I had been surprised that I had been healed without experiencing a sensation of tingling. I had experienced the Holy Spirit and had always felt a tingling. I thought this would be the same.

As Bob was driving home, I asked him, "When you were healed, did you tingle?"

"Are you doubting the Lord?" He asked.

"No. I just want to know if you tingled when you were healed."

"No."

But God had put sunshine in my life. He had healed me, with no tingling. *To God, be the glory.*

"Be delighted with the Lord. Then he will give you your heart's desires." Ps. 37:4

On Thursday I stopped taking the medication and canceled my doctor's appointment. I tore up the insurance forms for $1 million coverage.

Fourth miracle -- my grandmother's foot

In February of 1985, Gram was 89 years old and living at the Baptist Retirement Home in Maywood. She had never gone to a hospital for an illness or for surgery.

But Dr. Ronald McDonald, the physician for the retirement home, ordered her to be admitted to West-Lake Hospital in Melrose Park for a treatment of a festering sore on one of her heels that would not heal. It was then she learned she was a type 2 diabetic.

Dr. McDonald told her that the sore was gangrenous, and that unless it healed, he most likely would have to amputate.

Mother and I were with Gram, and I didn't like what I heard the doctor tell her. I did not want Gram to lose her foot. I became determined right then and there to pray with her and ask God to heal her.

I sat down to talk with her.

"Gram, do you believe Jesus can heal you?"

"Yes."

"Jesus is only a prayer away, you know," I said.

Mother and I went home, and I read what the Bible had to say about healings -- to call the elders of the church to pray over the sick person. But our pastor had left, and

I didn't know whom the elders were. So that wasn't an option.

But the Bible also said as Christians, we would be given gifts as needed. If you had the faith of a mustard seed, you could move a mountain. I had that kind of faith.

I prayed all night, and the next morning. "Please, Lord, heal Gram's foot; don't let her lose it." I learned that Mother had also prayed all night.

We went back to the hospital early the next day. I didn't have much sleep. I brought some baby oil to put on her forehead. Then Mother and I laid hands on her.

I said, "Gram, do you believe Jesus can heal you?"

She said, "Yes."

I said, "Gram, do you have any un-confessed sin? If you do, take it to the Lord now. We don't want anything to keep us from him."

She said, "No."

I put baby oil on Gram's forehead, and Mother and I started to pray. I had told Gram, "No matter what happens, know it is Jesus answering our prayer."

We prayed like we never did before. We prayed in the name of Jesus, to please heal this festering foot.

"Lord, please don't let them cut on her. We are asking you, Jesus, to heal her foot."

Mother and I started praying. We told Gram to expect a miracle.

After a short time, Gram said, "Oh, my God! My foot -- *it's burning.*"

"Gram, don't worry about the burning. It's Jesus healing your foot. Do you believe that?"

"Yes, honey, I do," she replied.

Mother and I continued to pray and thank the Lord. When we were done, I knew her foot had been healed.

I told Gram, "Let's just thank him for what he's done."

Mother said to me, "Do you want to look at the foot?"

I said, "No, I don't have to. I know Jesus just healed it. I could feel the Holy Spirit flow through my hands. Thank you, Jesus. Thank you, Jesus. Thank-you, Jesus," I said over and over. I was so happy I was crying and left the room.

Dr. McDonald passed me at the door, and I followed him back in.

He said, "Hi, Mabel. How's the foot doing?" He unwrapped the sheepskin bandage. He took hold of her foot and studied it closely, turning it this way and that.

"Why, where is the sore?" He said. "Maybe they wrapped the wrong foot."

He studied her other foot.

Then he looked again at the foot with the unwrapped bandage, then again at the other foot.

"I don't understand," he said, shaking his head.

I spoke up, "I do. Jesus healed it. Just before you came in, we prayed for the foot to be healed so you wouldn't have to do surgery today -- or any other day."

"No, we won't be doing any surgery. There's no need to."

Why did the healing occur? *We had the faith.* Not the seen faith, but the *unseen faith* to believe that what God says in his word is true. Gram was his child.

All things are possible with the Lord. Gram was his child, and we had the faith. Not the seen, but the unseen faith to believe that what God says in the word is truth. Not to be questioned.

That day changed Gram's life. I wrote the following poem about the incident:

Judith Neumann-Dicks

Re-birth

There was an old woman who sat in her chair.
She complained day in and day out.
Her age was 89, and her life was filled with grief.
Is it any wonder her words would only repeat?
"I don't have this
"I don't have that
"I can't do this
"I can't do that."
Till that day you brought her to the gate.
"Wait," you said.
"For you're not dead.
"I'd like to hear some praise.
"Have you no joy, no love to spread?
"Your life has been long days.
"Go back and wait.
"Fill your family and your friends with the joy
"I've given you.
"Yes, I'll take your pain, your grief.
"Now see what you can do."
The old woman turns 90 next week,
And her life is born anew.

Gram lived for four more years, to the age of 93. And to think she was once the little baby that everyone had thought wouldn't live more than six months!

Chapter 29
Marie

It was a recent Halloween; Len and I were being kept busy answering the door to pass out treats to neighborhood children. Their costumes seemed extra cute this year. There were practically every kind of costume one could imagine, and, yes, many little goblins and witches.

It was a tall girl wearing a black witch's dress ringing the doorbell that reminded me of Marie.

I met Marie back in 1972 while working at the PX (Post Exchange) at the Great Lakes Naval Training Center. I had just returned to the Chicago area (Hanover Park) from Washington, DC, where I had left David and had decided to divorce him.

I felt fortunate to get the Great Lakes job. It would put food on the table for Richard, Jacob, and me. I considered the job to be interim, while I looked for a better one.

When David had been based there in the past, we had an excellent baby-sitter for Richard named Ruth Kelly. She was a beautiful Christian black lady with seven children of her own. I contacted her and soon lined her up to baby-sit both Rich and Jacob.

Marie was from Jacksonville, Florida, and was living with a friend of her family. She was 19, tall, big-boned and, I might add, well endowed. By this time I was 26. We made a deal; she would move in with the boys and me and pay only $20 a week toward food and baby-sit the boys so I could date. This arrangement saved me additional money.

Soon I met a man who was willing to date on Marie's schedule. He was tall, good-looking, owned his own company, and was a lot of fun. He was 14 years older than I was but loved to do things with my boys.

It didn't take me long to learn that if ever I was going to marry again, it would *not* be him. He had been married before and said he would *never* marry again. I wanted more, and the time came to move on.

Marie and I worked out well as roommates. We were hardly ever home at the same time. She was dating a sailor at Great Lakes. Not only was she a Christian, but she also made it known that she was a virgin and was going to remain so until she married.

I soon quit my job at Great Lakes and got a job at the Lakehurst Mall managing a boutique shop. After about a year I heard of a job opening, managing some apartments in Schaumburg.

Marie decided to move out and move in with a friend. But that didn't work out, and it wasn't long before she moved back in with me. She had lost her sailor boyfriend and went into a deep depression.

Superwoman doesn't live here anymore

She wanted me to buy her car just so she could pay off her loan. I didn't need it, but I bought it anyway.

Then she decided to go home to her family in Florida. I agreed to allow her to leave a few of her belongings, a box and some hanging items, in my front closet.

Months went by and I didn't hear from her. I finally decided she would never come back.

In the meantime, I was managing the apartment complex and had just married Bob. A week later Marie calls from O'Hare International Airport.

"I'm home," she said. "I'm at the airport."

My mind whirled. What am I going to do with her? I quickly got an idea. Bob still had his furniture in his old apartment, and the rent had been paid for the month. I went and picked up Marie and settled her temporarily in Bob's former apartment.

Shortly thereafter, a friend named Fran was looking for a roommate. I decided that Marie and Fran would be perfect together. I sold Marie's former car back to her for what I had paid for it. I decided to keep the car in my name until it was paid off.

Marie met a young man in her building named Doug who was studying to be a minister. I told her she could use the car but not to loan it to Doug because I had seen his car -- it didn't have a square inch without a dent. Neither my insurance company nor I wanted to take a chance on his driving.

One of my friends came by and said he saw Doug driving the car. By this time Doug had moved to Oak Park and was working in Schaumburg. I tried calling Marie, but got no answer. I next went to his work to collect my keys. He didn't have the car with him that night.

Bob and I drove to Oak Park to retrieve the car. We arrived with the police just as Doug had arrived to move the car. We drove it to a friend's house, so if he had had keys made to it, he wouldn't find it.

I didn't trust Doug; we already had had two falling-outs. He didn't want his brother from Michigan living in his apartment. His brother decided to sleep in the apartment parking lot. One of the tenants came home after dark and spotted him sleeping in the car. When the tenant called me that night, I said to call the police. They did, and when the police arrived, they arrested him for an outstanding warrant from Michigan. This took place in Cook County, and now he would be going to Cook County Jail.

Doug was so mad at me he beat on my door and was yelling at me for having his brother arrested.

The second run-in was because he, Doug, had not paid his electric bill. The electric company had turned off his electricity. The maintenance man came to me and said Doug was stealing electricity from the complex.

I went to his apartment and saw an extension cord running under his door and plugged into the hallway outlet. Doug was shaving. I unplugged it and stood at his door waiting for him to come out to see who unplugged it.

I held up the cord and said, "Is this what you're looking for?"

He was mad as a hornet. I told him I would plug it back in so he could finish shaving but if I found it plugged in again, I would have him arrested for theft of service. I told him, "Don't try me." Soon after he moved.

Marie moved too, and the last I heard was that they were a couple. She never came back for the car, and I didn't hear from her for over a year.

When Marie was moving out of my apartment, I saw her taking a long black dress. I asked, "What's that?"

She said, "My boyfriend up at Great Lakes was in a cult, and this is my witch's dress."

I was shocked and said, "If you think you had problems before, as long as you keep that dress, they're just going to get worse."

She said her witch's name was sewed in white on the inside of the hem.

I was glad to see it go. If I had known before, it would have been gone a lot sooner.

Maybe that is why on Richard's sixth birthday, the cross and chain he had wanted disappeared on the same day he got it.

I had had no idea what Marie had gotten herself involved in.

Chapter 30

Al, Ward, and Joyce

The poor health of my brothers, Al and Ward, in the summer of 2008 prompted me to decide to have a family reunion. I scheduled it for Saturday, August 2, and sent out invitations to family members and friends.

I selected August because it was before Al's 72nd birthday. Ward's and Joyce's birthdays are in October.

Al had phoned me from his home in Urbana, Illinois, in the spring to say "good-bye." Al has diabetes, and had had his left leg amputated after several operations had failed. As if that wasn't enough, he recently had heart-bypass surgery.

I wrote a letter to Al, thanking him for being the best brother any girl could ever have.

Al's wife died of cancer two years ago in DeKalb. He has a son, Ward Phillip, and daughters Sandra, Alison, and Amy, and two granddaughters -- Kate and Emily.

Ward had been living in Acapulco, Mexico, for eight years, and his health had been failing. He and a friend had contacted E. coli on a weekend, and the friend died the following Tuesday. He also contacted the grunge from a mosquito bite (common to Mexico).

The reunion was a huge success. I had sent out 125 invitations; 88 family members came, and many friends.

Len and I held the party in our back yard. We had a tent and hired a musician who could play *80 different instruments.*

The party was fun. It helped us remember that we are a fun-loving and caring family. One of my friends said, "I can't believe how you all get along."

One of the highlights of the party was to pay tribute to Mother, who had died three years earlier. We made up a treasure chest of items Mom had left us, including a crown, because she had always called herself *the Queen.*

I told the story of how one Halloween I took Mother to the Addison Senior Club. When she saw another woman there dressed up as a queen, Mom said, "Doesn't she know *I'm the queen?*"

I replied, "I don't think we should tell her, Mom. But if she shows up at our meeting again dressed as the queen, then you should set her straight."

Al

Al went to college at Ottawa University, Ottawa, Kansas, and worked for the Boys Clubs of America. He also was a schoolteacher.

I remember Al as being like a butterfly -- he always seemed to be moving. He had Illinois jobs in Aurora, Naperville, and ended up in DeKalb.

Al and his wife, Pat, had an unusual relationship. After many years of a hectic marriage, they separated. They shared the children and never divorced.

I believe Pat was bi-polar. She would have mood swings ranging from manic to depressive.

Before we would go to their home to visit, we would call first to make sure they were going to be home. Mother would always look forward to the visits, giving her a chance to see her four grandchildren.

But when we would arrive, we'd find Pat hiding in the bathroom or bedroom, not wanting to come out.

Al would always try to make the best of it, but it was uncomfortable for us all.

Later they separated, Pat going to live with a friend. Al supported her until her death in 2006. Two daughters, Alison and Sandra, were living in California, and their son Ward and daughter Amy lived here.

Shortly before Pat's death, Alison came home to take care of Pat. This cost Alison her job.

Al was pretty sick at the same time. He had already had heart-bypass surgery, had his leg amputated, and had diabetes. Pat died after a long bout with cancer, with her entire family at her bedside. They had a graveside funeral. Her ashes were scattered in her yard under a tree that she had loved.

Pat's family didn't inform us of her terminal illness until after she had died. She was a very private person and wanted it that way.

I had drawn close to God in the last six months and really enjoyed creating beauty for the Lord. But I was tired, and the Christmas season had brought more work.

I was in my first marriage to Bob. We were going to have an open house on Christmas Day. Out of 34 who were invited, 17 came.

My cousin Steve went into the hospital in Chicago and was unable to be with us.

We had planned a turkey dinner the Thursday before Christmas for my brother Al and his family. But little did I know that suddenly life was going to get complicated.

Just as that turkey dinner for Al was being put on the table, the call came from DeKalb. Al had had a stroke and a heart attack.

Sandy, my sister-in-law, and Ken, her new husband, and three children -- Jennifer, Alison, and Karen came for the week between Christmas and New Year's.

My cousin Gary from Kentucky, where he lived with his wife and three children, had a pipe freeze, and as they sat and ate dinner, the pipe broke and sent 18 inches of water into their basement.

My son Richard's dog had 10 puppies.

My son Jacob was dating a new girl who had a jealous ex-boyfriend who was slashing tires on weekends. He slashed five tires in two weeks.

Bob was busy taking the wall down in our family room to re-insulate.

Ward

Ward Lee Smith was born October of 1938. He had been in the Peace Corps, serving in Togo, West Africa.

Before Ward was in the Peace Corps, he served in the Air Force. One of the places where he was stationed was Merced, California.

One of the things I remember about Ward was that he was very generous. Al had been attending Ottawa University, studying to be a minister and was home for the summer working at Brach's Candy Co. to earn money for school. He had hid his money in his Bible, and someone stole the money.

When Al didn't have any money to take with him back to school, Ward sent him some. Ward also helped Al get through various money crises a number of other times.

One story I remember about Ward was when he was a teenager; he went back to the old neighborhood in Chicago to see his friends. It was a Sunday when the park pool was closed, and he and his friends jumped the wall and went swimming. The police showed up, but Ward stayed in the pool, hiding under water until they left.

But coincidentally, Ward was having an appendicitis attack. When he returned home, Mom and Dad took him to the hospital for emergency surgery.

Superwoman doesn't live here anymore

That day stands out in my memory because Joyce and I were home alone watching a scary movie on TV. It was just getting dark when our cousin Betty came by and scratched her fingernails across the front screen door. Joyce and I screamed. Joyce and Betty were attending Carl Schurz High School at the time.

I also have fond memories of Ward driving me in his brand new Chevy Impala to the hospital when I was pregnant and about to give birth to Richard. I padded the front seat with towels and baby-wet mats to prevent my staining it.

With Ward driving, me in the front passenger seat, and Mother in the back seat, we arrived at West Suburban Hospital in Oak Park. Richard Anthony Largo was born half an hour later. It was November of 1967.

Ward married Sandy, who had been a close friend of mine. We would shop together, raise our kids together, and go to Bible study together. She was my trusted friend, and still is today.

Sandy and Ward divorced in the 1980s. She then moved to Minnesota and married a man named Ken.

Joyce

Joyce was born October of 1940, in a Chicago hospital.

Joyce and I used to play a game we called "dead man." We would undress down to our underwear and then re-dress each other in pajamas while we played dead.

Joyce and I got into a fight once, and she choked me until I passed out. She thought she had killed me. To this day I can't stand anyone's hands on my neck.

In September of 1959, Joyce was wed to Chuck Hudson. About 200 people attended the wedding at Irving Park Baptist Church on Irving Park Rd. in Chicago. We had been members there since we lived on Ridgeway.

They had been very involved in the youth group. They met at Avondale Grocery Store. Chuck's mother, Fran Hudson, was the cashier. Chuck worked in the butcher shop cutting up chickens and sometimes working with fruit and vegetables. Joyce and Cousin Betty would offer to go to the grocery store daily just to run into him.

Chuck joined the Army and was stationed at Biloxi, Mississippi. Joyce went with his parents to see him there. After he got out of the service, they were married.

His parents had moved to New Jersey, so Chuck was at our house for Sunday dinner most of the time.

Joyce was working downtown for some lawyers but gave up that job. Mother applied for the job and got it. They gave up their apartment and we (Mother and I) took it over.

After Joyce and Chuck married, they lived in Chicago for only a short time. They bought a ranch-style home in Hanover Park. Our visits to them were limited; we didn't own a car, and there were no buses.

Joyce and Chuck had three children: Cheri Lynn, who was blonde and had beautiful blue eyes, and David, who was as cute as he could be with a round face and chunky legs. Julie was born several years after David. She was a carbon copy of Cheri, but very shy.

They opened their four-bedroom raised ranch to Richard and I while David, my husband, was serving in Viet Nam. We were there for nine months. We (Joyce and I were both Christians) had the time of our lives. We went to church together, raised the kids together, went on picnics, and swimming outings. These events were a lot of fun back then. Chuck would come home and ask, "What are the ding-a-ling sisters up to today?"

We had grown very close, although there is a six-year difference in our ages. When I was in grade school, she was already in the working world. Then she got married and moved away. Mother and I were still in Chicago, just getting by.

Joyce and I still enjoy each other, even though miles separate us.

Chapter 31

Richard

I described Richard's birth in Chapter 16. This chapter will give a few highlights in his life. As you may recall, he was born November of 1967, while my first husband, and Richard's father, David, was serving with the "Seabees" in Viet Nam.

Richard was an adorable boy -- just as cute as can be, with brown, curly hair. He wore a smile most of the time. He had an innocence about him that absolutely glowed. He was enticingly huggable.

When Richard was about eight years old, one of his baby teeth came out, and that night he put it under his pillow, expecting a nice little reward from the Tooth Fairy. The first night: no Tooth Fairy. The second night: no tooth Fairy. And after the third night, again no Tooth Fairy, Richard stormed out of his room.

"That does it! I don't believe in the Tooth Fairy any more."

I asked him why he was so upset. He explained the situation. He forgot to tell me the tooth had come out, that he had placed it under his pillow.

"I lost a tooth three days ago, and it has been under my pillow for three nights, and she hasn't shown up yet."

I pulled him aside. "Don't let Jacob know. You see, when you lose a tooth, I have to put in a call to the Tooth Fairy to alert her. Put the tooth back under your pillow, and I'll make the call."

That night the Tooth Fairy showed up with 50 cents and a note:

Dear Richard,

I am so sorry you had to wait so long for me. But due to the seasonal rush -- baseball, soccer, and all, I've been very busy. I hope this will help. Enclosed is 50 cents.

Love,

The Tooth Fairy

The next morning he ran from his room with the note in one hand and the 50 cents in the other hand. "Mom, you were right. She did come, and she left a note. But how come when I lose a tooth at Grandma Largo's, I get a dollar?"

"That's easy," I replied, "your Grandma Largo lives in an affluent neighborhood."

"What's that?" he asked.

"That means the people in Grandma's neighborhood are rich."

He left the kitchen happy and took the note to school for show-and-tell. The teacher called me that afternoon. "I loved it! He was so proud of his note!"

I told her what I had told Richard about why the Tooth Fairy pays more in his grandma's neighborhood. She laughed and so did I.

I realize that Richard came by alcoholism rightfully. After all, both his father and grandfather were alcoholics.

At age 21 he showed such potential. He had a good job, bought a house, a truck, two cars, and a boat. He got married at age 23 to Lisa, whom he had dated for nine years. They were perfect together. They loved camping, boating, and fishing, but they neglected the most important ingredient: church.

Soon they began to party and go to bars, and that was the downfall of their marriage. They lost their dog, which accidentally hung herself on the chain-link fence. They drank more and more. He lost his beautiful wife. They both had taken the wrong path.

He sold his dream house after living through adding a second story in the summer when it rained every weekend for seven or eight weeks. This required the inside to be rebuilt also.

Lisa moved out, and the cars and boat were sold. All hope in his life vanished. Drinking took priority over all else. Between lawyers' fees, DUIs, "detox", and hospitals, I thought for sure I was going to lose him. He even had a seizure and bit into his tongue.

Superwoman doesn't live here anymore

Richard is a very good-looking man, and ladies are always flirting with him.

About five years ago, I thought he had hit rock bottom. Len and I were at church when we met Manny Mill at his prison ministry. I was impressed by what Manny had said, and I bought a copy of his book, *Radical Redemption*. Rich read it and said he just had to meet this man.

The following week we went to a church in Wheaton. The battle for Rich's life was on -- between good and evil.

Rich stopped at a gas station and drank a bottle of vodka on our way there. During the service, Rich got up and went to the bathroom twice to vomit.

When the service was over, Manny and three other men were going to pray. Finally, I thought, "Lord help him (Rich)."

The lady and her kids who clean the church after the service were making noise and climbing over the men to pick up papers. Manny realized it and said, "Why don't we pray over in this other room."

It was the library. Not much better for privacy. The Holy Spirit came over Rich, and God zapped him good. He signed into a home: Wayside Cross Ministries in Aurora. He lived there for a year. They had Bible studies daily, computer courses, and Rich even went on to college.

I thank God for giving Richard his life back. I know he will do well in his ministry. I was thrilled. He got a job with an ex-minister. I thought, I've got my beautiful son back. When he is sober, he glows.

When Richard was 12 and Jacob was 8, Bob and I drove them to Virginia to meet up with David, their dad. He was stationed in Cuba and had invited them to spend a month with him there. After leaving the boys with David, Bob and I returned to Hanover Park.

When we left the house to go next door to return some electric timers we had borrowed, our dog, Peppy, a miniature black poodle, saw a big white dog across the street and darted out of the house. Hurrying across the street, Peppy was struck by a car and killed. Rich and Jacob truly loved her, and I wondered how I could ever tell them she was dead.

After being with their dad in Cuba for a month, I drove to O'Hare to meet them. They arrived with their stepmother, Carol, David's wife. I had dreaded this day when I would have to tell them Peppy was dead.

On the way home from the airport I decided to tell them right away and get it over with. Rich took it hard.

That night I overheard Rich say, "Jacob, get down on your knees with me. We are going to ask Jesus to give us Peppy back. It says in the Bible that he can raise people from the dead. So, why can't he raise our Peppy from the dead?"

I would never question Rich's faith. He knew God in a very real way. He was right, and I wasn't going to dash his hope. He had the faith to believe it. I was proud of him that he was willing to pray for her return.

A few days later I spotted an ad in the newspaper. It read, "Lost miniature female poodle, black, 8 pounds, found in Evanston (Illinois)." It listed a number to call.

I phoned and said, "I know this is not my dog, but if you don't find the owner, would you please sell her to me?"

The lady on the other end said, "You can have her now. I've run this ad for a month, and no one has claimed her. She is really cute. In fact she is better than the poodle we own. But my kids would kill me if I gave ours away and kept her."

I said, "Come on, boys, we have to go pick up something."

Rich and Jacob had been praying for their dog's return.

They didn't ask, and I didn't say where we were going. We arrived in front of a big, old Victorian house with a long front porch and wide steps going up to the porch. Through an oval glass in the front door, you could see the two dogs in the kitchen.

I rang the doorbell. A woman came right away, followed by the little dog, which looked exactly like Peppy.

Rich and Jacob dropped to their knees, and the dog jumped up and licked their cheeks. Rich ran his hand down her belly and then looked up at me. "This isn't Peppy, Mom. This dog has eight nipples. Peppy only had seven." One of Peppy's nipples had never developed.

Were they ever thrilled when I told them we were going to take the dog home and love her and, of course name her Peppy. The new Peppy lived many years with us.

Chapter 32
Jacob

Jacob, as you recall, was born in September of 1971, at Bethesda Naval Hospital, four years after Rich. Just refreshing your memory a bit -- Jacob's twin died at birth, and I hemorrhaged so much during the deliveries I almost died.

When Jacob was about eight years old, he asked me one day, "When did God make the world in color?"

The question caught me off guard, and furthermore, seemed rather strange. Before I answered I said, "Why are you asking?"

He said, "Because all the movies and cartoons on TV are in black and white."

"Oh," I said. "It was probably in the 1960s. God said, 'Let there be color, and it was.'"

At age 34, Jacob still hadn't married and was living in Denver with a friend whose name was Norm. It was a rather strange arrangement. Jacob is an organized "*neatnik*", and Norm -- well, a mess. Two opposites. Not unlike the TV pair, Felix and Oscar.

Jacob had dated a lot of different women but had never found the right one. That is, until he went back home in Illinois to attend a friend's wedding. He met an old girlfriend, she's now a high school teacher, and they started cross-country dating. It wasn't long before they were engaged and married. Just like that.

Eighteen months later, my granddaughter was born. She was a beautiful blue-eyed girl. She looked just like Jacob did when he was born. She could have been declared Jacob's clone.

My grandson was born in February of 2009, about 18 months after my granddaughter's birth. He looked a great deal like is big sister.

Jacob moved back to Illinois and got a job as a technical writer. Jacob and his wife were quite busy raising their daughter, getting ready for the new baby, and tending to two dogs and two cats. But the job they are doing raising my granddaughter tells me they are very fine parents.

When Jacob was 18 months old, Bob and I took both boys and our friend Fran out to diner. Jacob, sitting in a high chair, patted the waitress on her behind. She quickly turned and said, "Who did that?" Jacob then pointed to Bob. The waitress said, "No he didn't. That was you. That was a little boy's hand."

Jacob was known for crashing my car. He and I had a lot of time at home without a car during his teen years.

One day at dusk, Bob and I returned home a day early from a vacation and found a party going on at our house. Painters' tarps were spread over the carpeted areas. The music wasn't too loud, and Jacob had everything under control. It wasn't a bad party -- nothing to be ashamed of.

Another time Jacob bet the next-door neighbor's son $5 he could dive off the second-floor railing into their pool. We ran over, and Jacob had already dove in.

Coming up out of the water, he shook the water off his face and opened his eyes. I said, "Hi, Jacob."

"Mom!"

"It's time for you to come home, Jacob."

"Be there as soon as I get my $5 back," he said.

Jacob had been working as a bouncer at several nightclubs in downtown Chicago. Then he decided he needed a lifestyle change when he witnessed a shooting outside one of the nightclubs he had worked at. He moved with a friend to San Francisco. Jacob moved back to Illinois shortly after Bob past away. He wanted to be here for me, if and when I needed him. A few years later after I met Len, Jacob knew I was in good hands so he moved to San Diego, and a few years after that, to Denver Colorado.

Before Bob past away, I couldn't just go visit Jacob; we couldn't afford that. He did well to make friends -- lasting friends, with families.

After Bob died, Rich and I drove out to San Francisco and we had a great time sightseeing with Jacob.

Jacob asked if I needed him at home since Bob died. I said No, even though I would have loved for him to be there. He had made a life for himself; I didn't want to mess it up for him, but he moved back anyway.

He now lives 20 miles away with his wife, his daughter, and son. He is a Christian, and I am so proud of him.

Chapter 33

The Last Vacation

As December (2008) approached, we were looking forward to our annual vacation. We own four time-shares in Mexico, which we bought several years ago. There are two different plans, points, and weeks. We get two weeks for each unit to be put in a bank, and when we pull them out, we can use them anywhere in the world. This time we were going to use them in Florida for 10 weeks in a row.

Len has owned two condos in St. Petersburg Beach since 1976. They are two studio apartments that face the Gulf and have the most beautiful sunsets. We planned to stay there all of January (2009) and then move on to Kissimmee, Florida, using the weeks for all of February and half of March.

This would be a first for us, as the longest we had stayed away was a month. The winter seemed unusual as far as snow in the north goes, so we made plans to go south. In the past Len's brother and wife have stayed in the other unit in January, but this time they were waiting on the results of a biopsy. So we would go it alone.

My son Jacob's wife was pregnant and due in February, and this would be my second grandchild. I didn't want to be away, so I booked a flight back to Chicago for his birth. Normally we would leave the day after Christmas, but for some unknown reason, we stayed home until January 4.

It takes us two days of driving, and we were off on our 1,224-mile trip. We timed it right; the weather was beautiful for travel. When we got to St. Petersburg Beach, the temperature was 80. This lasted about a week, and then the temperature went into the low 70s.

The afternoon we arrived, we shopped for groceries -- $84 worth -- and returned to the condo and put them in the refrigerator.

The next morning, we discovered that the refrigerator was not working. Len had owned several units in another part of town, and we had purchased four refrigerators and two stoves in the last three years, all from Sears. It was evening when I realized the refrigerator wasn't going to get any colder after turning it as low as it would go and putting all the groceries in the freezer.

We looked up the Sears Service Center in St. Petersburg and set about to call for a repairman. Len started the call and after half an hour of getting the runaround, he passed the phone off to me. It wasn't long before I realized I was talking to a man in India. His English was hard to understand, and because our past purchases had gone to different addresses, I was asked four times for my name, address, and the contract number. I gave him the address four times for where we needed service.

I told him we didn't have a contract that we were looking for a repairman to come out and repair a refrigerator purchased three years ago.

"What is the brand?" He asked.

"Galaxy," I said.

"We don't sell that brand."

"You did three years ago," I said.

I tried so hard to make my point and grew more and more frustrated by the minute. I finally said, "Would you please get your supervisor? I really need someone who can help me."

I heard a click, followed by loud music. I sat there holding the phone to my ear, listening to that music, as though I were hypnotized. About every 10 minutes Len would say, "Why don't you just hang up?"

I prayed that I would keep this professional and not get loud or nasty out of frustration.

After about 40 minutes a voice came back on the line. I truly believe it was the same man, asking my name, address, and contract number yet again.

After I answered all of his questions, he said it would be a week before a repairman would arrive.

I told him, "That's not good enough; I'm going to take our business elsewhere."

Superwoman doesn't live here anymore

The next morning we called the number of a local repair service. Four hours later the refrigerator was up and running.

Bob and his wife, Shirley, who live in Ocala, Florida, had a call from Boston that Nana, his 95-year-old mother, had died. He and Shirley were leaving on a cruise the next morning with their daughter, son-in-law, granddaughter, sister-in-law, brother-in-law, son, and new wife, who had given them the cruise as a 50th wedding-anniversary gift. If they cancelled, they would ruin the trip for all of them.

In the meantime, Bob's sister went ahead and had the funeral without them. I know it must have hurt him, as he was close to his mother. She would stay with them every year for four or five months at a time.

She was a beautiful lady with white hair who carried herself well and dressed to the nines. Not only was she loved, but she will also be truly missed.

I felt we really needed to make the effort to stop and see them. Shirley insisted we not only come but also stay over in the guest room in the home they had lived in for eight years without a guest because whenever we came through, Nana was there for the winter.

Shirley has a very heavy Boston accent. *Pahk the cah.* We went, and we stayed, and had a great weekend.

Shirley is a fine cook, and Bob has lots of stories from his working for United Airlines. He was in charge of booking travel for sports teams. When it comes to service, he was the right man for the job. Now he golfs, and she is the Queen Mum for the Red Hat ladies.

We had been out for brunch, and Bob was making a map for our return to St. Petersburg Beach when Len's daughter Michele called. She had been to the post office to pick up our mail. I answered the phone.

"I'm afraid you have a problem here at the house," she said, referring to our house in Addison, Illinois. "Your hot water tank ruptured, and the furnace, being next to it, sucked it up and burned out the circuit board. You have no heat, the temperature inside the house is 24 degrees, and all of the toilets and water pipes are frozen."

My mouth dropped. I waited for her to say "April Fool!" But it wasn't April.

"I've already called a plumber and a furnace-repair man. They're on their way over."

Len and I knew Michele was capable of handling it, but she said on Tuesday she would have to return to work.

Our minds started to race. We wondered: How is it possible for water to "run up" and put the furnace out? And, what happens when the thaw comes. Will the pipes break? Will the toilets break?

It was bedtime. Len slept, and my mind was back in Addison inside our house.

When we woke up in the morning, Len's breathing machine stopped working. He has to have it at night for his apnea; his breathing stops every 60 seconds.

Me -- I made up my mind that we needed to return home, and I had a panic attack. This was a first for me, because I was usually good under pressure and would fall apart later.

Well, I was a mess. The room was spinning, and I couldn't stand up. My stomach was whirring, and Len was saying, "Now, we *have* to go home. I can't sleep without the machine."

He packed and loaded the car; we were on the road by noon heading back to Addison.

This brought back memories of the year before last when the furnace had gone out and Michele had discovered it. But that time, Len was at the hospital after falling and crushing three vertebrae in his back. We went home early that time, too, and had the furnace replaced.

On the way home, we hit a rainstorm in Georgia and missed our exit by 30 miles. Turning around and going back the 30 miles added an extra hour to our trip.

We didn't sleep well that night, and I was up at 3 a.m. We had stayed at this Best Western before and knew it had a nice breakfast. We arrived in the lobby at 6 a.m. for breakfast but a sign said, "Breakfast at 7 o'clock." During our previous stays, it had been "Breakfast at 6 o'clock."

We were making good time that early in the morning. The weather was overcast but great for driving.

Things went well until in Indiana a truck kicked up a rock that hit our windshield. Or, had it been a bullet? We had passed a car ahead of the truck, and I happened to gaze at the driver, who returned a very mean stare.

We thought we would be home by 3 o'clock that afternoon. But as we exited I-294 to I-290, we had a blowout in the rear driver's side tire. Len pulled as far off the road as he could, but traffic was so close and so heavy that to change the tire was impossible. We would have been killed.

We called Michele and asked her to please send a tow truck to us, but to make sure it had a flatbed trailer to pick up our car. In the meantime, the "minutemen" came by, offering to change the tire for us. We told them we had our trunk full, and that we had a tow truck on the way.

Then two Mexican men stopped and offered to help, but we thanked them, telling them we had a tow truck on the way.

It wasn't much longer before a tow truck arrived with a big, blue, flatbed trailer. By the time we got into his front seat, the driver had hooked the car and had it onto the back of the truck.

Once back on the highway, it wasn't but a short ride before we arrived home. The plumbing trucks were in our driveway. Steve, Len's son-in-law, had his truck parked in front along with Michele's car parked out in front.

It was so nice to be home, but we wondered what we'd find inside. The plumber was finishing up, and Michele was paying him.

There were painters' tarps in the living room, along with our patio set and lots of lamps and odds and ends in the dining room. Downstairs, the family room furniture was stacked to the ceiling in one corner of the room and plastic painters' tarps covered everything.

The ceiling had a large hole in it that had been cut to release the water that had gathered and caused a large bow. That ceiling hole brought a new discovery: bees, bees, and more bees. There were cones left behind from thousands of bees that had invaded the house over 20 years ago. They were all dead, but very present.

The pipes above were exposed, because the pipes on the second floor were the ones that broke. The workmen were leaving the ceiling and walls open to dry out. If we were to close them up too soon, we would end up with deadly mold. The wool carpet below was wet, stained, and it smelled.

The hot water tank was replaced in the utility room next to the two-year-old furnace. The water tank was what started the trouble. When it ruptured, it poured water over the floor, and the furnace, being next to it, turned on and sucked the water in until it shorted out the circuit board. This left the house with no heat. When the temperature dropped to 24 degrees in the living room, it left an 8-foot crack across the hall ceiling.

Our belongings were stacked on every possible square inch that was dry in the family room. There were stains on the rug outside the powder room door. I had just had a hardwood floor installed in this room.

There was evidence that water had poured down from above and across the powder room floor and into the hall (at the bottom of the stairs).

Now for the trip upstairs -- there was dirt on the stairs, all the way down the hall and into our bedroom. There was the hole, 2 feet wide and 5 feet long, in the wall plaster, and plaster dust in front of it. This wall backed up to the master bedroom bath.

The pipes were exposed; some were shinier than others. The caps on top were replaced, along with a pipe that connected to our shower.

When we left on vacation, I had the house spotlessly clean. Every time we leave for a trip, I always clean my way out of the house. Len would always say, "Why are you cleaning so thoroughly? Are we having company?" This was something I would always do; it always felt so nice to come home to a clean house.

Our next-door neighbor had been shoveling the snow off our walk while we were gone. We had the mail and newspapers stopped. We had asked our neighbors to keep their eye on our house while we were gone. I had asked my son Jacob and his daughter to stop by on Sunday and check on the house and let her run through the rooms. She is 18 months old and was to become a big sister in February (of 2009).

I had purchased a ticket to fly home from Florida on the day the baby was to be born and then to fly back to Florida to finish our vacation.

Michele had already got the ball rolling with the insurance company. She put in the claim, and two days later we got a call from a very rude adjuster, who accused us of not being responsible while going on vacation.

This wasn't true, because we have an alarm system, we had the mail and newspaper stopped, and we had arranged to have the snow cleared off our sidewalk.

We had installed a new furnace. But who would have guessed that the water heater would blow?

Once we got the clean up under way in earnest, it seemed various workmen were always in our home. It was back and forth with paint chips to the Home Depot and Lowe's. The plaster and painter came in from Wisconsin and stayed overnight. The carpet was picked out and waiting for the painter to finish. The furniture was so big, and it was being given to the painter. The carpet was laid the very next day.

We hadn't told all the groups we are involved with that we wouldn't be home. I told Len; this is our vacation, so let's dedicate our time to putting the house back together.

We took my car and drove up to replace Len's breathing machine. Wouldn't you know it? The car overheated!

We took the car in to have the tire replaced and had to wait a day for the correct size tire to arrive. A year earlier we had paid $600 for four Vogue tires. Now, they wanted $250 for a *single* tire. The next day we took the car that I drive to have the radiator flushed.

Finally, we thought we had both cars up and running. Not so.

Thursday night is garbage night, and we had a lot of garbage. I was helping Len carry a mirror from one room to another when it hooked onto an electric cord, slipped, and broke. If we believed in bad luck, this might have affected us for the next few days, but it didn't. The mirror went into the garbage with the carpet, mattress, and old TV.

The time quickly came for Len and me to go to the hospital to await our new grandson's birth. We arrived and saw my daughter in-law being taken to the delivery room. When we entered the pre-delivery room, there were Jacob, his daughter, his mother in-law, his sister in-law with her son who was 9 years old; and now, Len and me.

Giving birth today is so different as compared with when my two sons were born some 40 years ago. I don't think the change is a real improvement. In fact, I find today's birthing procedure very stressful. It's a real joy to see a newborn, but I think the mother deserves less confusion and more rest -- more time to hold and examine her new baby before anyone else does.

We went back the next day, but, once again, I believe the visits should be short and sweet. I had a plane ticket to fly in from Florida and stay in Illinois for four days and then fly back to Florida. But I was already home, due to that house emergency.

I had owned a five-piece entertainment center that was 12 feet long. The painter brought in a trailer and hauled it away. The carpet would be installed on a Monday morning. The carpet-cleaning service would be there that Wednesday, and the new mattress would be delivered on that Saturday. I had bought cabinets to replace the entertainment center. To save space, they were being installed in a closet. Len and I were doing this on our own.

We were feeling as if it had all come together and the work was done. It was Valentine's Day weekend, and we enjoyed Thursday with Jacob and his family, and

Saturday we took Michele and Steve out to dinner. This was the second weekend in a row to repay them for their help in our disaster.

We celebrated my birthday two days ahead of time. Rich had called to wish me an early happy birthday. I was hurting and felt like the next birthday would be my 100th.

After a restful weekend, Monday was my birthday. For years my sons would celebrate it on the 12th, so they wouldn't get it mixed up with Valentine's Day.

Our troubles were not yet behind us. On February 16, I got up early and started the dishwasher. Then I headed for the laundry room to put some clothes in the washing machine. That's when I discovered that the sewer was backing up onto the laundry room floor.

My brother Ward called from Mexico to wish me a happy birthday. I had to shut down the washers, get the water turned off, get the furnace shut down before the water got in there.

Waking Len to the mess and keeping the water away from the new carpet was a challenge. It was 8:30 in the morning when I called the plumber to rod out the same drain we had had rodded out last November. Here we go again. I had bought a new dishwasher and refrigerator at the end of November. The old refrigerator had stopped working, and the dishwasher was filled with sewage water. I never wanted to use it again.

We had installed a new dishwasher, and thank goodness its water was filling up nice and clear.

When Len called the plumber, he was told the plumber wouldn't be able to arrive until 2:30 in the afternoon. All that time we couldn't flush a toilet or turn on the water. And -- we had a dinner date at 5 o'clock with our gourmet-dining group. This is about a dozen seniors who get together once a month for dinner. I had intended to invite all of them to come back to our house for dessert. The group surprised me with an orchid.

The plumber finished rodding at 3:30. Now it was time to bathe and get ready for that dinner date. Both of my sons phoned after we left the house for dinner. Rich called back when we got home. Next, my sister Joyce phoned. She was in Florida in the time-share that we couldn't use. They had left the previous Wednesday to avoid a snowstorm that was headed toward Illinois. Joyce simply could not believe all the troubles we were experiencing.

On the very next day, we were scheduled to entertain blind veterans from the Hines Veterans Hospital, who would be arriving by bus to the Addison VFW, where we would be cooking them a dinner, followed by playing bingo with them. The dinner menu was to be barbecued beef sandwiches, fries, coleslaw, pickles, with apple pie and ice cream for dessert.

We enjoy doing this for them once a month. Actually, one month we entertain the blind veterans, the next month the disabled veterans, and the third month, the veterans with addictions.

We are calling this our last vacation, but it might not be -- only time will tell. We hope never to have another one like this one.

Sitting back and relaxing after all the cleanup and repairs were completed, an 8- to 10-inch snowfall had just begun. This was the kind of thing we had hoped to be in Florida to avoid. I'm reading poetry and getting ready to prepare Italian meatballs for an open house at our church.

Chapter 34
Deaths

The deaths of loved ones, relatives, and friends almost always leave an indelible mark in one's memory. I have already covered the deaths of Mr. Neumann, Aunt Elsie, Daddy, Mrs. Neumann, Aunt Gerry, Bob, Jim, David, and Mom and also, my stillborn son. Following are the deaths of two very special friends: Barbara Hanson and Michael Suty, who were an important part of my life.

But first, sometimes relatives or friends ask me to give a eulogy at a wake or funeral service. Each time I pray beforehand that whatever I say will glorify the Lord.

"Lord, this is for you. Show me what to say." He always fills me with confidence, and the words roll out. I've not had any formal training at public speaking, but I have done a lot of it since I was a little girl.

Barbara Hanson
October 21, 1995

Barbara was a dear friend from church. Her children did not know the Lord, which had been her heart's desire. I wrote the following about Barbara at 4 o'clock in the morning on October 22, 1995, after learning of Barbara's death. I was asking the Lord why he woke me. Whom did He want me to pray for? He was leading me to write the following remembrance:

God's Family Album

Treasured Memories and Reflections of Barbara Hanson

We (Bob and I, and my Mom) have been friends with Barb and Arnie for about 12 years; we attended the same church. We also belonged to Gideons at the same time. We would have dinner about twice a week with Barb and Arnie. We were also in a Bible study group together for many years. Barb and Arnie have been my prayer partners over the last three years while my husband, Bob, went through cancer. Bob was given the word about two weeks ago that he is in remission. Although I ask for your prayers for my neighbor, who has had cancer since March, she has been going in and out of a coma as of yesterday. The doctors give her approximately two months to live. Her name is Shirley Karp. Please pray for her.

Love, Judy.

Pictures from the Family Album

I brought with me this morning a picture album, pictures of Barbara's life. Many of her friends have treasured memories and reflections. I'd like to share these with you this morning. As we go through this journey together, I would like you to see her as we did. She was born long before ultrasound but long after the Bible.

The first picture is found in *Psalms 139:13-16*. "You made all the delicate inner parts of my body, and knit them together in my mother's womb. Thank-you for making me so wonderfully complex! It is amazing to think about. Your workmanship is marvelous -- and how well I know it. You were there while I was being formed in utter seclusion! You saw me before I was born and scheduled each day of my life before I began to breathe. Every day was recorded in your book!

A Picture of Special Gifts and Abilities

The second picture I have of Barbara in my mind's eye that I'd like to share with you is -- she had many gifts and many abilities. These were very special. She had the gift of hospitality. When you entered her home, she could make you feel as if you had been there before. She had the gift of calligraphy. She used to write on the bottom of pictures and give them out as gifts. She had many arts and crafts that she was involved with. She made a house a home for Arnie and her. She was a great cook!

1 Corinthians 12:4-7 "Now God gives us many kinds of special abilities, but it is the same Holy Spirit who is the source of them all. There are different kinds of service to God, but it is the same Lord we are serving. There are many ways in which God works in our lives, but it is the same God who does the work in and through all of us who are his. The Holy Spirit displays God's power through each of us as a means of helping the entire Church."

A Missionary

Barbara was a missionary. No, she didn't serve in Africa; she didn't go to South America. She served on her mission field right here in this community. And every time she entered a store, restaurant, or hospital, she brought New Testaments and tracts, and sometimes a pretty little basket decorated to look very inviting. She would share at every opportunity.

2 Corinthians 5:11: "It is because of this solemn fear of the Lord, which is ever present in our minds, that we work so hard to win others. God knows our hearts, that they are pure in this matter, and I hope deep within, you really know it, too.

A Woman of Prayer

In my fourth picture here, it is a picture of Barbara in prayer. She prayed for her family, she prayed for her grandchildren, she prayed for her waitresses and restaurant workers, she prayed for her dear friends. Many times she was able to share these prayers with Arnie. When he wasn't available, she would share them with others so that we would continue to pray with her.

Matthew 18:19-20: "I also tell you this -- if two of you agree down here on earth concerning anything you ask for, my Father in Heaven will do it for you. For where two or three are gathered together because they are mine, I will be right among them."

A Woman of Faith, She Believed in Miracles

Barbara was a woman of Faith; she had the faith to believe that God was working in our lives. She had the faith to believe God was working in her own life, and she experienced miracles. When the doctors came to her quite a while back after they had experienced a house fire and told her they were going to amputate Arnie's hands, she said, "No, the Lord has told me He's going to heal my husband." And He did!

When Barbara heard Pastor John was run over by a forklift in California and was near death, she was on her knees.

She prayed for her grandson -- as a baby he had many medical problems. She called him her "miracle baby"; she had prayed, and God answered her prayers.

Hebrews 11:13: "By faith -- by believing God -- we know that this world and the stars -- in fact, all things were made at God's command, and that they were all made from things that can't be seen."

A Woman Who Knew God, and God Knew Her

Barbara was a woman who knew God, and God knew her. She didn't stop at sharing.

Psalm 139:1-5: "O Lord you have examined my heart and know everything about me. You know when I sit or stand. When far away you know my every thought. You chart the path ahead of me, and tell me where to stop and rest. Every moment, you know where I am. You know what I am going to say before I even say it. You both precede and follow me, and place your hand of blessing on my head."

A Picture of Barbara Praising the Lord

I picture Barbara praising the Lord, of which she often did, because she saw those answered prayers.

Psalm 146:1-2: "Praise the Lord, Yes really praise Him. I will praise Him as long as I live, yes, even with my dying breath."

A Woman Not Afraid to Die

Barbara was not a woman who was afraid to die, for she was prepared. She had prepared her heart ahead of time. She had accepted the Lord. For she knew in advance that she would someday die. When the doctors came to her last Monday and said, yes, it is cancer, they expected her to wake and quake, but she didn't. Instead, she said, "When can you remove it?"

2 Corinthians 5:1-5: "For we know that when this tent we live in now is taken down -- when we die and leave these bodies -- we all have wonderful new bodies in heaven, homes that will be ours forevermore, made for us by God Himself, and not by human hands. How weary we grow of our present bodies. That is why we look forward eagerly to the day when we shall have heavenly bodies which we shall put on like new clothes. For we shall not be merely spirits without bodies. These earthly bodies make us groan and sigh, but we wouldn't like to think of dying and having no bodies at all. We want to slip into our new bodies so that these dying bodies will, as it were, be swallowed up by everlasting life. This is what God has prepared for us and as a guarantee, he has given us His Holy Spirit."

2 Corinthians 5:7: "We know these things are true by believing, not by seeing. And we are not afraid but are quite content to die, for then we will be at home with the Lord."

Looking to Heaven, the Greatest Gift

In my next picture of Barbara, it is of her looking to heaven. The greatest gift. No, you can't buy it; no, you can't earn it. And you can't do anything here on earth to get to heaven on your own power. It is only through Jesus Christ Himself, by accepting him into your heart that you can get to heaven. It is a gift.

Matthew 5:6-7: "Happy are those who long to be just and good, for they shall be completely satisfied. Happy are the kind and merciful, for they shall be shown mercy. Happy are those whose hearts are pure, for they shall see God. Happy are those who strive for peace -- they shall be called the sons of God. Happy are those who are persecuted because they are good, for the Kingdom of Heaven is theirs."

A Woman with Desire

In my last picture of Barbara, I picture her a woman of desire. She had a great desire to win others to the Lord. She had a great desire to see those of her family to come to know the Lord in a special way, then they would be able to spend eternity with her.

James 4:7: "So give yourself humbly to God, resist the devil, and he will flee from you. And when you draw close to God, God will draw close to you."

Just recently Barb expressed that when she died, she didn't want us to be sad, but rejoice, because she'll be in Heaven, and it just can't get any better than that!

Thank you & love,

Stay in touch, you'll be in my prayers.

Judy Neumann

Michael Suty
February of 1996

This was my eulogy for Michael Suty:

In the past 42 years that Arlene and I have been friends, we have shared many joys and many sorrows. Today being one of sorrow. As a family you will experience a greater loss, but as friends we can sympathize, love, and hold you up in prayer. It seems almost fitting that I eulogize Michael Suty, who died on the day I was born.

Yesterday I heard that Michael had served in World War II and fought in the Battle of the Bulge. More recently, he entered the hospital and lost his battle for life last Friday. He was unable to fight any longer.

When we are born into this world, we never stop to think that death is the only way out.

What I'd like to share with you is that that doesn't have to be the end. That Jesus Christ allows us hope for the hereafter, eternal life. The scripture says that when we are absent from the body, we are present with the Lord, for those who love the Lord. In 2 Corinthians 5, it tells us, "For we know that when this tent we live in now is taken down --- when we die and leave these bodies, we all have wonderful new bodies in heaven, homes that will be ours forevermore, made for us by God Himself and not by human hands. How weary we grow of our present bodies. That is why we look forward eagerly to the day when we shall have heavenly bodies which we shall put on like new clothes. For we shall be spirits without bodies. These earthly bodies make us groan and sigh, but we wouldn't like to think of dying and having no bodies at all. We want to slip into our new bodies so that these dying bodies will, as it were, be swallowed up by everlasting life. This is what God has prepared for us and as a guarantee, he has given us His Holy Spirit."

2 Cor 5:7 states, "We know these things are true by believing, not by seeing. And we are not afraid but are quite content to die for then we will be at home with the Lord. This is a written guarantee that comes with a free gift. "Our Salvation." It can't be bought, you can't earn it, and in fact you can't do anything to get to heaven on your own power. To receive your gift, you must go before the Lord and open your heart, ask for forgiveness of sins and follow the Lord, not looking back to the old ways. If you desire to know that you will be in heaven for eternity, this simple task can be done today.

During the last days of Michael's life, he was fortunate enough to have a nurse who knew why Jesus Christ came to this world as an infant, died on a cross for our sins, rose on the third day, and sits at the right hand of God. But before he went to heaven, he left us his Holy Spirit to dwell in those who ask for forgiveness and ask him into their hearts. It is in this grace that the free gift of salvation is given.

The nurse, Maria Lopez Cortez, did not know your dad until recently, but she did know God, and she knew her job was to share with Michael and give him an opportunity to accept the Lord Jesus Christ in his heart as his personal Savior, if he hadn't already done that.

Today I asked Arlene (Michael's daughter) if I could speak to you. (I had met Arlene in the fourth grade, and we had stayed in contact for all the years until his death.

Our paths had crossed many times over.) You see, my father died several years ago, and I don't know if I will ever see him again. He didn't have a Maria Lopez Cortez at his bedside. Perhaps he did cry out to the Lord at that last moment. I don't know; his life didn't include the Lord.

There is a song by Dave Boyer, "If you were arrested for being a Christian, would there be enough evidence to convict you?" Well is There?

The Lord is called the Comforter. He gives peace when none is to be found. He gives hope when all looks hopeless. Yes, he will give joy after the sorrow. One of the things that I recall hearing about was the rock collection gathered by your mom and dad stored under the bed. Having lived on the third floor, I had a real concern for the people on the second floor. You won't be able to look at a rock without special memories. I know I won't.

Many years ago while living on an island and experiencing a storm, I was told that the palm trees can be blown over and bend almost all the way to the ground and not break because their root systems grow deep through he sand and attach themselves to a rock. That's why they are able to survive the worst of storms and spring back up.

The Lord Jesus Christ is known as the rock of salvation. Wrap your roots around him, and no matter how rough the storms get, you'll still be standing when it's over. The greatest inheritance you can ever receive is the Lord.

Let us pray.

Chapter 35

No More Superwoman

So you see, I used to think I was *Superwoman* -- that I, Judy, could handle any and all of life's blows on my own -- without help from anyone -- including God. But life taught me that I was wrong. Boy, was I wrong.

As you can readily see in this book, life dealt my Superwoman a fatal blow. Kaput! She wasn't very "super" after all. In fact, the woman I thought was Superwoman was actually nearly helpless and desperately in need of God.

That's why, when I turned my life over to God, my Superwoman status vanished. I didn't need that moniker anymore. But in my new status, with God always at my side, now I am actually a million times stronger than I was as Superwoman, because now, God is my partner. I no longer try to handle the big stuff; I let God take care of it. God lets me handle the small stuff, which he has adequately equipped me to deal with.

Yes, I tossed out my Superwoman cape years ago, and not too soon either. Now God is my Superwoman cape.

Isn't that just too exciting for words? Now, with God as my partner, we as a team can handle anything.

ANYTHING!

So can you. Get rid of your Superwoman cape. Partner with God. He's BIG. He's STRONG.

He wants you. He's waiting patiently for you to invite him into your life as your partner.

Go ahead. Do it. Invite him in.

I sincerely hope that something in this book will help you to know the Lord, our Father in heaven, who is waiting for you to ask him into your heart.

"However, I consider my life worth nothing to me, if only I may finish the race and complete the task the Lord Jesus has given me of testifying of the gospel of God's grace." *Acts 20:24*

Judith Neumann-Dicks

Judith Neumann-Dicks wears a number of "hats":

- Prayerful Christian
- Mother of two sons
- Grandmother of 12 (2 natural and 10 step grandchildren)

In addition, she is active in the following organizations in Addison, Illinois:

- Seniors Club
- VFW Post 7446
- Senior Police Academy and its Community Emergency Response Team (CERTS) and Volunteers in Policing (V.I.P.)
- The Addison Court system, directing people to the courtroom
- Addison Gourmet Group

She is involved in the following church-related groups:

- Grace Community Church (formerly Keeneyville Bible Church)
    - Past Bible Study leader
    - Wedding coordinator
- Bloomingdale Church
    - Past Prayer Team member
    - Past Grief-Support leader

And she is active in these additional groups:

- Glenhill Lunch Bunch, Glendale Heights, Illinois
- The former Glen Oaks Hospital Grief-Support Group, which meets in her home

LaVergne, TN USA
12 November 2009
163918LV00004B/2/P